READER'S VERSION®. C
reserved throughout the work

New Living Translation (NLT)

Today's New International Version (TNIV)

ISBN: 978-0-9893971-0-0

Book Layout Designed by Indie Designz

Printed in the United States of America

Table of Contents

Introduction

Have you ever gazed into the mirror and cringed at the reflection staring back at you? Have you ever wished you could be someone other than yourself? Do you ever wish your confidence were stronger or felt as though you were drifting through life without a sense of purpose? Do you often see the negative in everything—especially yourself? If you answered yes to any of these questions I have a message of hope and encouragement written just for you.

While writing the opening chapters of this manuscript several years ago, I was completely broken in spirit and confused about love, life and my purpose for living. My self-esteem was at an all-time low, and I was consumed with feelings of worthlessness and inadequacy. I had just relocated across the country from San Jose, California to Baltimore, Maryland, to begin nursing school. With no family or friends nearby and still healing from the remnants of a broken relationship feelings of isolation and loneliness surfaced. Consumed with feelings of despair, hopelessness, insecurity and self-hatred, I found little solace from the quiet thoughts that raced chaotically through my mind. During those lonely hours, I questioned my existence and asked, "Why would God allow such a simple and worthless soul to remain in existence?"

The loneliness brought a time of solitude, which compelled me to deal with my unresolved issues. It was just the Lord and I. I could no longer run from the pain and hurt I had tried to ignore for more than half of my life. During those private hours, the tears fell endlessly as I poured my heart out to God, pleading for an ounce of relief from the sorrow that overwhelmed me.

The inward struggle I faced with self-hatred started during my early childhood. As a young girl growing up in a predominantly white neighborhood with few children who looked like me, I was filled with thoughts of inferiority, mediocrity and insignificance. I couldn't see the beauty in the dark hue of my complexion or appreciate my own uniqueness when other children criticized my appearance. The constant ridicule of my skin color triggered the desire to be someone else. As a young girl, I found it difficult to handle these inner struggles, and they followed me well into early adulthood. It wasn't until years later that I came to realize how God used these painful experiences to help mold me into the caring, compassionate and unselfish person I am today.

Working as a registered nurse has opened my eyes to the frailty of life. So many patients come into the hospital with life-changing health conditions, like terminal cancer, debilitating injuries, paralysis, tumors, painful malignancies, kidney failure, limb amputations . . . and the list goes on. Seeing the strength, courage and resilience of my patients has affected me more than I could ever have imagined.

I often reflect on times when patients were alive and recovering one minute and no longer living the next. I now realize life is simply too short to waste time feeling sorry for ourselves. God has strategically placed each of us on earth for a purpose. However, until we can love ourselves unconditionally and move beyond feeling insignificant, we will never be able to carry out our life's mission effectively.

This book began as a heartfelt journal entry and evolved into a healing manuscript that has pulled me out of the whirlpool of low self-esteem I was drowning in for over half of my life. After praying and speaking with other women, I discovered I wasn't the only person searching for ways to deal with an identity crisis. In a world that measures people by their fame, fortune and fashion, it's easy to become consumed by superficial goals and images. We often forget who we are, a part of God's amazing creation and made in his image and likeness.

I pray that this book will help you on your journey to healing. I pray these words will inspire you to look past your faults and to love yourself the way God loves you—simply, just the way you are. I pray each chapter encourages you during the lonely hours of life to speak hope into your situation and ignites a flame inside that empowers you to walk in the purpose God has for your life.

Getting Past the Ugly is designed to be read as a daily meditation over a one-month period. Each day builds on lessons from the days before. Each day's reading is interactive, offering a scripture of the day, thoughts for reflection, an affirmation and a plan of action. As you read the daily thoughts, prayerfully ask God for his strength to complete the journey. Take one day at a time and always remember, "The fastest runner doesn't always win the race, and the strongest warrior doesn't always win the battle," (Ecclesiastes 9:11).

Life is not a sprint but a marathon. It requires endurance, patience, and a determination to succeed. Keep a journal of your thoughts and feelings as you go through this healing process. Recite the affirmations aloud because, "Faith comes from hearing the message," (Romans 10:17 NIV). I also encourage you to meditate on the daily Bible scriptures. Always remember you are not alone in this process—God is walking with you every step of the way.

I pray this message helps you to see who you already are—loved by God without condition. I pray it not only transforms your view of yourself but also enables you to move past the one thing that has stunted your growth and hindered you from fulfilling your God-ordained purpose in life. That one thing is . . . YOU!!!

Be Blessed!

With Love,

Bermesola M. Dyer

First...
A Prayer for the Reader

Lord, help me to get this message out to those who are struggling with who they are and the way you created them. Use me as your vessel to encourage someone else's soul and to minister to her spirit. Someone needs to know we find our beauty within and it's the little things we do every day that make us who we are. It has little to do with the external or what we look like on the outside. Someone needs to know that the value in who we are has nothing to do with what others think of us but has everything to do with how we value and perceive ourselves.

Give me strength to be transparent as I expose some of my most intimate and personal thoughts, thoughts I have kept hidden for so long, too ashamed to reveal to others. Give me courage to expose my fears and hurts and the truths that I have learned along the way.

Let this word that you have placed in me be the saving grace for that soul on the brink of disaster. Let this word be a light to the one embodied in a world filled with darkness. Let this word be the healing balm for the one who has been hurt by what others have said about her or what she has said about herself. Lord, invoke abundant life into the spirit of your child and help her grasp the reality of Christ's unconditional love. Help her know that because you love her completely, you call her to love herself the same way. Bring her a new understanding of beauty and bring wholeness into her existence. Let her know that receiving your love and simply loving herself are enough.

Transform . . . Inspire. . . Reform . . . Revamp . . .
Rejuvenate . . .

Enable her to get past the ugly and

Recreate the understanding of beauty...

the beauty of self-love!!!

Acknowledgements

I would like to begin by thanking my friends and family for their support, encouragement and patience throughout this laborious process. Thank you for listening to my ideas and offering your candid insight on how to bring everything together. Your feedback has been invaluable and I truly appreciate the love you've shown me.

To my sister girls: Kashe Ferguson, Odessa Balumbu, Courtney Clendinen, Clarissa Cherry, Zakia Brunson and Andrea Parara. Your friendships have played an indelible role in this voyage called womanhood. Thank you for your genuine spirits, your listening ears and your wonderful words of advice.

To my confidant and best friend Steve McFadgen: Thank you ...for everything! I couldn't have prayed for a better bond.

To Leslie Anderson of Women and Girls All That: It was almost 15 years ago I attended that Women's Weekend retreat and heard the God-inspired messages that would change the course of my life. Because of your willingness to follow God's lead, and host that conference, my life and so many other women's lives have been transformed. Thank You!

To my business partner and friend Danushca Pardo: God has blessed you with an amazing gift of creativity and innovation and I am truly grateful for the opportunity to bring our gifts and talents together to make our world a little better and a little brighter.

To my editor and coach Angela Dion of Dion Communications. Please accept my deepest...deepest gratitude for your patience, your encouragement, words of wisdom and understanding. Thank you for helping me charter through this new territory and empowering me to find the courage I needed to step out in faith and follow my dreams. You didn't give up on me and the end is finally here!

To Karen Burkett of Christian Editing Services: God has a way placing the right people at the right time into your path to ensure his will is accomplished. I am sincerely grateful for your services.

Special thanks to my Spiritual Shepherds and Pastors including: Pastor Horacio Jones of Fremont Bible Fellowship, Fremont, California; Pastor Bob Jackson of Acts Full Gospel Church of God In Christ, Oakland, CA; and former Pastor Willie T Gaines of Emmanuel Baptist Church, San Jose, CA. Your God-inspired messages have sustained and kept me during the fragile moments of life.

To Pastor A.R. Bernard of Christian Cultural Center, Brooklyn, NY, thank you for the series "A life of Purpose," I'm no longer "chasing donkeys" but fulfilling God's purpose for my life!

To my present pastors, Bishop Alfred A. Owens and Co-Pastor Susie C. Owens of Greater Mt. Calvary Holy

Church, Washington, DC. Thank you for your leadership, guidance and encouraging words throughout the years. Bishop: Thank you for teaching me the importance of prayer, faith and perseverance. Co-Pastor Susie: Thank you for teaching me how to be a woman of God and the importance of loving myself no matter what! Your words have been truly inspiring and I will always keep them dear to my heart.

And lastly I would like to thank my Heavenly Father for placing this vision in my heart and enabling this book to come to fruition. For over 5 years I struggled to put the words and message of this manuscript together but you were patient and wouldn't let me walk away from this assignment. You persistently pushed me out of my comfort zone and empowered me to step out in faith. Thank you for the doors you've opened and paths made clear. It's for you I live and for you I die. May the words I say and the things I do be pleasing in your sight and may my life's work sing a sweet melody to you.

Dedication

This book is dedicated to my parents Devon and Caroline Dyer, who have been a constant support throughout all my endeavors and helped me become the woman I am today. Thank you for teaching me how to love God, showing me how to love others and inspiring me to love myself. Dad, your steadfast and praying spirit is unprecedented. Mom, your relentless hope and faith that is larger than a mustard seed has truly moved mountains. Words cannot express how much I appreciate your love, your patience, your guidance and the wisdom you have instilled in me throughout the years. I am forever grateful!

May the following poem encourage and inspire you to find
your own strength during this journey.

Resilient Woman

Her eyes gaze into heaven as her soul shudders with pain.
The sting of life's lessons has scarred her will to fight.
Yet her heart fixed on hope and her spirit determined to
overcome, she presses on . . . she presses on . . . she presses on.
Why?
Because her strength is in her arms.

Though her journey seems endless,
she presses on . . .
Though her stride is interrupted by the potholes of life,
ensnared by traps set along the crooked path,
she presses on . . .
Why?
Because her strength is in her arms.

The strength in her hands bears the weight of her sorrow and
she finds the will to continue through the hope of tomorrow
hill after hill. Mile after mile . . .
Through scorching sun, thunderous storms, treacherous terrain,
and endless battles she presses on . . .
Through closed door after closed door, heartbreak after
heartache, failures, tragedies, disappointments and setbacks, she
presses on . . .
Why?
Because her strength is in her arms.

Her only option is to fight.
Failure is not an option.
Retreat is not an option.

Surrender is not an option.
Why?
Because she's found strength in her arms
Hope in her heart
Healing in her mind
and a spirit of resilience that defies all odds.

Bermesola M. Dyer, 2009

My grace is sufficient for you, for my power is made perfect in weakness. Therefore I will boast all the more gladly about my weaknesses, so that Christ's power may rest on me.
2 Corinthians 12:9 (NIV)

I can do all things through Christ who strengthens me.
Philippians 4:13 (NKJV)

Day 1:
Lord, Help Me Love Me!

How would you describe the reflection you see when you look into the mirror? Would you say she is an intelligent, gifted, beautiful, confident woman filled with potential? Or would you describe her as an out of shape, average, insignificant, woman in need of help?

If you've ever seen yourself negatively, know that God doesn't see you in that manner. He created you, uniquely in his image and you are an extraordinary individual. He has a plan for your life and wants to help you see yourself as he does. Perhaps past hurts, disappointments or unreachable expectations others have placed on you have blinded you. If this is your story, God wants to heal your vision and help you love yourself past the pain. He promises you can do all things because Christ will give you the strength.

Any healing process begins by admitting we have a problem and need help. If you are reading this book, you are on the right track to getting the help you need. You have probably become well acquainted with your insecurities and the dissatisfaction you have with your self-image. If you are looking for words of encouragement to guide you to a place of love and acceptance and a way to make peace with your shortcomings you've come to the right place ...keep reading.

For more than fifteen years I struggled with self-hatred. At the age of nine, I learned I was ugly from the boy who sat beside me in school. He often asked me irritating questions like: "Why are you so dark? Why is your hair so nappy? Do you know you remind me of a burned piece of toast and a crispy cream doughnut?" The children on the school bus confirmed his sentiments and called me names like "Tar-baby," "Blackie," and "Buckwheat." The girls in the locker room taught me I was skinny and underweight. They often referred to me as "Olive Oil," "Skinny Minnie," and "Bones." I also learned I was poor from the snickers of my church friends when they discovered my parents took me shopping at the Salvation Army and Goodwill.

I didn't recognize how great an influence my childhood experiences had played on my young adult life until one day, at the age of 19, as I stared disdainfully into the mirror I came to the revelation that I hated who I was. As I gazed at my reflection, I began to scrutinize every inch of my body. I hated the dark and uneven skin covering the frail skeleton of a frame. I couldn't stand my hair because it was too thin, too short and way too kinky. My nose was too big. My butt was too flat. My lips were too full. Feet too long...head too big...and the list went on. The situation got so bad that at one point a single look in the mirror led to an overflow of tears. During my darkest hours, thoughts of suicide surfaced, and I prayed for God to remove me from this earth.

One night the Lord heard me gasping in distress. I cried out with a broken spirit and desolate heart, "Lord, I need your help! Please, help me to love me! Teach me how to love me the way you love me because I can't do it without you!" That night he came to my rescue, but it was only after I acknowledged I had a problem far too great to solve on my own.

When I started pouring my heart out to the Lord, the healing began. Sometimes all it takes is asking for help to receive the miracle that's been waiting all along. Recovery begins with acknowledging you need help; asking for the help you need and then being willing to receive that help from God. The Word of God says, "You do not have because you do not ask," (James 4:2 NKJV).

What do you want God to do for you during this journey? What do you want to accomplish by the time you finish reading this book? Don't be afraid to ask for his help and allow him to show himself strong in your life. He's willing and able and wants you to live an abundant life. Jesus said, "I have come that they may have life, and that they may have it more abundantly," (John 10:10 NKJV).

I pray you will open your heart to receive all God has for you. He will give you everything you need to be the person he's called you to be. This process starts by believing you are his child and knowing that he loves you unconditionally.

During this journey you will experience an array of emotions as you reflect on your life and all the experiences that have led you to where you are today. You may be tempted to suppress your feelings and hide the hurt, but you cannot bring healing to your wounds if you do not allow them to surface. God will help you through the pain if you allow him. He is your resting place. Let him carry you through the fragile moments, and he will transform you into a stronger, wiser and better person. It has only been by the grace of God that I can now look at myself and truly believe that even with my flaws, I am a beautiful woman. It is my prayer that you reach that place too.

Affirmation: I have been equipped with the tools I need to overcome my struggles. With Christ's help and strength I will accomplish all I desire to accomplish during this process.

Action: The Word says to write the vision down and make it plain (Habakkuk 2:2) and without a vision, people perish (Proverbs 29:18). What is your vision for this 30-day journey? Where do you see yourself by the end of the book? What do you want to accomplish? In other words...what is your mission? Write your goals down and place them somewhere you will see them every day. This will enable you to remain focused on the mission you must accomplish and encourage you during the difficult road ahead.

Here's an example to help get you started . . .

By the end of this 30-day journey, I will begin to see myself through God's eyes. I will find it easier to love myself unconditionally. I will begin to discover or reconnect with my purpose for life and begin walking in that purpose and helping others along the way.

For as he thinketh in his heart, so is he.
Proverbs 23:7 (KJV)

For we wrestle not against flesh and blood, but against principalities, against powers, against the rulers of the darkness of this world, against spiritual wickedness in high places.
Ephesians 6:12 (KJV)

Day 2: Get Ready for War

Before we go any further, I caution you to be prepared—this transformation will not be easy. I don't want you to think that by the time you finish this book your change will be complete. This is just the beginning and it will be an all-out battle that will demand your time your patience and commitment. So get ready to embrace this life-changing process; it will bring you one step closer to reaching your mission complete.

Your journey to healing will be physically draining, emotionally taxing and spiritually trying. You are well aware of your ailments and shortcomings and in the past may have allowed them to shape your self-image. Perhaps you have focused on them instead of the reason and purpose God created you. Or maybe you have focused on what others have said about you instead of what God says in his Word about you. Healing requires a change in your thinking, so the real battle takes place in the mind. Changing the way you think will be the most difficult but critical portion of the healing process because that is where your inspiration and motivation begins.

The mind is the joystick for the entire body. It tells the body what to eat, what to wear, how to feel and how to respond to circumstances. As a result, when our thoughts are in disarray, our entire body is out of sync as well.

Your thoughts control your actions. Understanding this element and deciding to do something about your mind-set will help you take the necessary steps to move forward on this journey of healing. By beginning this quest with a positive attitude and a determination to succeed, you can expect a victorious outcome. You can have whatever you say; you can be whatever you think you are. If you want to change your circumstances, then set the change in motion by changing your perspective. You have to change the way you think.

American societal norms suggest that beauty equals perfection. To be beautiful you must have flawless skin, the perfect silhouette and flowing tresses. Society also equates power and money with success. Often other people place unreasonable expectations on us. They want us to be or do what they think we should be or do—which may be very different from what God has planned for us. Unfortunately, many have fallen victim to these unrealistic and misguided expectations. They do everything in their power to reach these superficial goals, but what happens when they don't measure up? Could this be the reason so many girls and young women are suffering from low self-esteem, anorexia, bulimia and obesity?

This battle will require you to deal with the real you—naked, vulnerable and completely exposed. Perchance you are in the midst of an abusive relationship or still dealing with the remnants of one that destroyed your self-image. Or maybe you aren't measuring up to someone else's idea of success and you see yourself as a disappointment. Whatever you are dealing with, this is your opportunity to bring closure to your past and begin preparing for your future.

To begin healing and moving towards God's kind of success, you will need to align your thoughts with the Word of God. Proverbs 23:7 reminds us, "For as he thinketh in his heart, so is he," (KJV). In other words, you are what you think. If you think you are unattractive and undesirable, then guess what? You are unattractive and undesirable. If you say you are a beautiful person with a beautiful spirit, then you are a beautiful person with a beautiful spirit. Remember, you are exactly who you say you are, and you will have exactly what you say you will have.

The word of God tells us that God spoke to those things that were not as though they were. In other words he spoke the reality he wanted into existence. The first chapter of Genesis reveals the story of creation and it started with God saying "Let there be light...and there was light!" You were created in the image and likeness of God, so even if you can't see yourself being in a different situation at this time begin to speak the change you want to happen into existence. Use the power you have in your words to change your circumstance and to reach the goals you've set out to achieve.

As this pilgrimage continues, stay positive and persistent. Don't become discouraged. Continue to press forward no matter how much pain or hurt surfaces. Do not entertain debilitating thoughts or retreat when challenges come. Hold on for dear life and remember why you decided to take this voyage. Know that you will succeed in the end, and your life will be better as a result.

"For I know the thoughts that I think toward you, saith the LORD, thoughts of peace, and not of evil, to give you an expected end" (Jeremiah 29:11 KJV). What is God's expected end for you? An abundant and victorious life! Jesus said, "I am come that they might have life, and that they might have it more abundantly," (John 10:10 KJV).It is God's will that you walk in the fullness of life and overcome the spirit of low self-esteem. It's time to walk in the abundance of life! Are you ready?

God has blessed you with the gift of choice. You can choose to live or choose to die. You can choose to move forward, to move backward or remain stagnant. You can choose to love or hate yourself. You can choose to reflect on positive thoughts or negative ones. The choice is yours.

Are you ready to live? To move forward? To love yourself? To appreciate the good in your life? Your determination will define your success. How determined are you to make these changes happen? Are you ready for a new you? Then develop a new way of thinking, a new attitude. Commit to the changes needed and do not allow your mind to stop you from continuing on the path to recovery—and loving yourself.

Put on your war clothes and get ready because there will be a battle between your heart and mind. Your thoughts will tell you that you can't make it, you can't do it, you're not good enough and you're wasting your time. Let your heart push you past the doubt and fear.

Never lose sight of what you want to accomplish in this process. Review the goals you have set out to accomplish daily. This will remind you where you are now and where you desire to be. Don't let anyone or anything distract you from reaching your goals. Stay on course. Success requires you to take steps. Stay focused and directed because there is too much at stake to give up.

Affirmation: I am destined for greatness. I will achieve any challenge that presents itself. The battle is not given to the swift or to the strong but to those who endure until the end. Today I will prepare my mind for war. I will not waver or stagger when challenges come. I will remain steadfast and focused on reaching the goals I have set out to achieve.

Action: Write a letter of encouragement to yourself in your journal. State why you are determined to make it through this healing process and what tools you will use to help bring you through.

"For the Lord does not see as man sees; for man looks at the outward appearance, but the Lord looks at the heart."
1 Samuel 16:7 (NKJV)

Day 3:
This Is You Now

D o you often find yourself staring in the mirror, scrutinizing every flaw and imperfection? If you look hard enough, you can find 101 things wrong with your body. *I'm too fat...too skinny...my butt is too big...my butt is too flat...I'm too tall...I'm too short...too light...too dark...my nose is too long...my feet are too big...my hair is too thin...my eyes are not blue...look at all these stretch marks...* Sound familiar? These were some of my own sentiments throughout my adolescence and young adult life.

You might be thinking that I'm going to discourage you from any negative thoughts or self-deprecating comments today. Well...Surprise! Although it may seem strange, today is your day to do some "Body-Bashing." It's time to inflict yourself with verbal and mental grief until you can say and think no more. Today you can scrutinize, criticize, judge, complain, condemn, cry, scream, shout and talk about everything you hate about your body.

Go ahead…Get it out…Get it all out now! You have a mole in the most peculiar spot and you hate it! Or a glaring birthmark that is working on your last nerve! You're the shortest person in your family—scream about it! You feel as though you've failed at everything you do or you just can't seem to please those you care about. Why me? This is your opportunity to criticize yourself for everything you want to be but cannot be and everything you desire to have in life but have never been able to acquire.

I know this is unconventional and probably makes no sense. But part of this process involves examining who you are right now before concentrating on who you are trying to become.

This journey will not only require you to reflect on the present you and on your future hopes and dreams; it will also entail devising a plan and taking action in order to achieve the goals you originally set. Throughout the book I will suggest action steps at the end of each day to help you through this process. Today's step empowers you to take action by writing down the detrimental self-perceptions. Use this opportunity to be completely honest with yourself. Who are you…really? Devise a list of everything you don't like, wish you could change, wish was different and anything else on your heart. We will revisit this list later.

Use the sample comments at the beginning of today's entry to help you get started. Most likely, once you begin, the words will flow. If you don't like what you see in the mirror, than say it. If you wish you were someone else, than say so. If you wish you had more money, were smaller, shorter, taller, spoke more eloquently, weren't so shy, or so obnoxious, write it out; place all of your insecurities on the table.

Remember, I wrote this book to help me navigate through my own healing process, so I have already done many of the exercises I am suggesting. Here's an entry from my journal:

Bermie's Journal Entry: July 17, 1999

You know, I hate to admit this, but I have some serious issues! Everything in me wishes I could look different. I hate that I was born with such dark skin. It seems as if the girls with a lighter complexion, long hair and light eyes get all of the attention from the guys. If I'm walking with one of my friends who happens to be lighter than I am, I notice the guys always look at her first. They smile at her and barely glance at me and keep walking. Or they may stop us to talk to her and not even acknowledge me. It feels as if I don't even exist. It really hurts to feel like you're not valued and appreciated. Maybe if I looked different, things wouldn't be so bad. If I had the opportunity to change the way I look, here are just a few of the things I would ask God to redo:

1. My skin color (I want to be light caramel . . . who wants to be dark chocolate—ugh!)

2. My complexion (I want perfectly clear, smooth skin all the time. I get too many breakouts.)

3. My forehead (I want a smaller forehead. My hairline starts too far back.)

4. My breasts (Who wants a 36B? Lord, give me a 36C—full cup, please!)

5. My hair (I want longer, thicker, and fuller hair and I want it bone straight. My hair is thin and nappy.)

6. My height (5'7" is cool and everything but 5'11" would be better. Then I could be a model.)

7. My nose (I want a smaller nose—mine is too big. I feel like a parrot with this big honker!)

One of my greatest challenges during this exercise was standing in my own truth. I knew what I thought and how I felt, but I didn't want to admit it to myself or to express it to anyone else. Writing my private thoughts out on paper was also unnerving as the risk of someone else finding these hidden secrets in my journal would be devastating. What if they discovered how deep my pain was and that I hated my very existence? What if they discovered how insecure I was? What would they think of me? Would they hate me too? Despite all of these fears, I continued to write because it was my form of therapy and it helped bring me to a place of healing. As a result, this book was born from a heartfelt place that allowed me to express my pain and release the disappointments bottled up and festering inside me.

You may be inclined to worry about what other people think of you but this is all about you right now. The words you write today will be what you use to build your future. Once you've written down the negative thoughts, don't wallow in them. You can now move on. Commit to guarding your mind from negative thinking. After you've done this exercise, surround yourself with uplifting and encouraging messages. From this point on, there will be no more self-induced hatred through negative thinking or speaking.

Finally, brethren, whatever things are true, whatever things are noble, whatever things are just, whatever things are pure, whatever things are lovely, whatever things are of good report, if there is any virtue and if there is anything praiseworthy—meditate on these things. Philippians 4:8 (NKJV)

It's easy to envy someone because of her beauty, money, talent, life, education, intellect, charisma, athletic ability, or whatever else. At first glance, you might be inclined to look at another women and think she has the perfect life—and then desire to possess what she has. Be careful when making assumptions and speculations. Someone who appears to have everything together on the outside may be broken and hurting on the inside. The one thing you hate about yourself may be the one thing someone else wishes she had. You envy someone else's hair while the same person envies your smile. You want her hips and she wants your legs. You love her life and she wants yours.

Sometimes it appears the cliché is true, the grass is greener in someone else's yard. Appearances don't always reveal the truth. What seems appealing on the outside may be broken and dying on the inside. People don't always disclose what's going on in their personal lives and can purposely mask the hurt and brokenness they are experiencing. Begin to look at yourself from the inside out. This is the way God sees you. He's looking at your heart, your thoughts and your actions. He is more concerned about your spiritual attributes than your physical features. He's more interested in you being a healthy and spiritually sound individual than being a supermodel or the next big star. Take some time to reflect on your thought processes. Are you focusing more on your external appearance than on what's going on inside?

Affirmation: Today I graciously love myself from my inner core to my outer shell.

Action: In your journal, briefly describe your self-image. Talk about the things you don't like and wish you could change.

I don't mean to say that I have already achieved these things or that I have already reached perfection. But I press on to possess that perfection for which Christ Jesus first possessed me. No, dear brothers and sisters, I have not achieved it, but I focus on this one thing: Forgetting the past and looking forward to what lies ahead, I press on to reach the end of the race and receive the heavenly prize for which God, through Christ Jesus, is calling us.
Philippians 3:12-14 (NLT)

Day 4:
The Past That Haunts You

Another step to healthier self-esteem is acknowledging your past and committing to move beyond it. Release the skeletons in your closet and allow the painful memories you have been holding back to become exposed. Some of these memories may be so traumatic they have scarred you, stunted your growth and hindered you from moving on with your life. Maybe these scars have affected you so deeply that the wounds still feel fresh and you've been unable to heal; despite your efforts to suppress the pain, it is still a constant reminder of your past.

Perhaps your scars are the result of verbal or physical abuse, molestation, rape, backstabbing, gossip, abandonment, infidelity, and many other hurts or disappointments. Whatever the cause may be, acknowledge those experiences and face the emotions that surface as a result. This is a difficult step, but by not addressing the past, it will continue to haunt you and prevent you from moving on with your life no matter how deep you suppress those feelings.

You can't change what happened yesterday, but you can change how you allow yesterday to shape your future. For some people, the past is a crutch to lean on and an excuse not to excel. For others the past is a heavy weight that keeps them down and prevents them from achieving their ambitions. To still others the past is a stumbling block that causes them to second guess their potential and underestimate their greatness. Others use the past as a defense to justify their failures. For me the past was a ghost that continually haunted me and played games with my mind, causing me to doubt my potential. My childhood consisted of constant ridicule, isolation and feelings of inadequacy which followed me into adulthood, making it difficult to appreciate my value and walk in my purpose. How has your past affected you?

Perhaps a close loved one abused you and you have carried the hurt from the experience for many years. Or maybe, like me, people ostracized and ridiculed you because you looked different from everyone else. Perhaps people you looked up to rejected you and turned their back on you when you needed them the most. Whatever your situation, don't be afraid to face these problems, talk about them, accept that they happened. Confront the emotions that have surfaced as a result. These emotions might include rage, hatred, anger, mistrust, bitterness, jealousy, depression, guilt and a host of other feelings. Deal with these emotions and allow yourself to move on without the restrictions of your past.

Don't let your past define your future. Your new start begins with asking Jesus to forgive you for the mistakes you've made. Forgive yourself, and forgive others who have hurt and disappointed you. A few days ago you set goals on where you would like to be emotionally thirty days from now. Are you determined to make these goals a reality? Realize that your history is behind you. You can now look forward to defining your future story.

In today's scripture, the apostle Paul tells us how he dealt with his past mistakes. Before coming to know Christ on a personal level, he hated Christians and persecuted them because of their faith. After receiving Christ, he served him fervently—and in return, people treated him in the same malicious manner he had treated the Christians. Because of his faith he was beaten, ridiculed and imprisoned unjustly. He could have wallowed in guilt over previous sins. He could have dwelled on the hurt and rejection and the unfair treatment he received. But if he had chosen that path he could never be all God had called him to be. He knew he could not fulfill his purpose if he was distracted or controlled by his past, so he said this, "Forgetting the past and looking forward to what lies ahead, I press on (Philippians 3:13 NLT)."

What about you? Are you ready to forget what happened in the past and press on to what lies ahead? You can't put the past behind if it is buried within you. It's essential to acknowledge your past failures and setbacks.

Only then can you give them to the Lord and allow him to forgive your sins and heal your pain. Only then can you begin to see yourself as he does—a unique and extraordinary woman with a God-given purpose to share with the world.

Affirmation: Today, I acknowledge my past and will use it to propel me to a brighter future. I love myself beyond my past and into a new reality. My past does not define my future. I decree and declare that my future is filled with endless opportunities.

Action: Reflect on your most painful experiences and write a letter to someone who has hurt you. Describe how you survived the experience and how it made you a better person. What attributes and qualities have been strengthened and what lessons have you learned as a result? You can choose to mail the letter if it's appropriate, but writing it is more of an exercise for you to express the hurt. This will allow you to move beyond its stronghold on your life.

Each day we make decisions that affect the rest of our lives. The choices we make will often determine our successes and failures. I wrote this poem during one of my darkest hours to help me overcome a difficult breakup. I hope it encourages you.

Choices

Today I can choose to love myself...or despise my very existence.

Today I can choose to squander away precious moments, moments I will never see again...or I can choose to appreciate the one life I have to live and make the most of every day.

Today I can choose to feel sorry about my situation and accept it as reality...or I can choose to fight to reach the outcome I desire.

Today I can choose to believe that all hope is gone and that my circumstance has overtaken me...or I can choose to believe that no matter how impossible a situation may appear, nothing is impossible for the God I serve.

Today I can choose to believe I will never escape my financial woes and allow the fear of being broke to consume my health, peace of mind, and well-being...or I can choose to work toward achieving a prosperous future. I can remind myself that God wants me to prosper and to do well in life. God wants to bring me to an expected end.

God came so I could have an abundant life, but I must determine my fate.

I can choose to look at the bottle as being half empty or as being half full.

I can choose to be dejected and miserable or I can choose to be happy and satisfied.

I can choose to hold a grudge and to hate those who have hurt me, allowing the hate to fester, burn, and eat away at my soul…or I can choose to forgive those who have done me wrong and allow the healing process to begin.

Today I can choose to fight life's journey, repeat my mistakes, and continue to get bruised and battered from fighting…or I can choose to embrace the struggles of life and accept and learn the lessons they bring.

So what if I've made some mistakes in life! Who hasn't? My mistakes cannot and will not define me.

I can choose to stay back, go nowhere and remain in the same rut I've been in forever…or I can choose to bounce back from my mistakes and move forward with my life.

Today I can choose to listen to the skepticism and doubt from critics who have told me I'm worthless, unattractive, insignificant and will never succeed…or I can choose to believe I am more than a conqueror and I can do anything with the help of Christ because he strengthens me.

With all the good and the bad that surrounds me and so many important decisions to make…

Today I have a choice. What will I choose?

Bermesola M. Dyer, 2009

God causes everything to work together for the good of those who love God and are called according to his purpose for them.
Romans 8:28 (NLT)

Day 5:
The Past That Heals You

The past influences who we are today and we often make future decisions based on our previous experiences. If we are not careful, our negative experiences can stunt our future growth; but our painful past does not have to hold us back. In fact, God can use our negative experiences to propel us to a better future—if we will follow and trust in him.

God can bring good out of the most negative circumstances. Today's verse tells us that no matter what we go through in life, we can take comfort in knowing it will work out in our favor if we trust the Lord and follow him. When you are struggling with pain and hurt, it can be difficult to see how God could ever bring good from the experience, but he can. Trust in him, and he will bring you through every circumstance you face.

Yesterday we looked at Philippians 3:12-14. The apostle Paul encouraged us to let go of what happened in the past, to continue pressing forward to reach our goals and to fulfill the purpose God has for our lives. Now that you've acknowledged your past and the experiences that have shaped you, pray for strength to accept your past despite being unable to change it. Although the truth of your past will always exist, you have the power to change your outlook and the way those memories will shape your future.

Are you ready to stop dwelling on the hurts and begin looking for the good God has promised to bring from them?

Maintain a positive outlook and know that no matter what you've gone through, God has already worked out the end results to be in your favor. His word affirms, "'For I know the plans I have for you,' says the Lord, 'plans for well-being and not for trouble, to give you a future and a hope,'" (Jeremiah 29:11 NLT). So instead of beating yourself up, holding grudges, suppressing painful memories, and allowing those memories to keep you in bondage, use those experiences to take you to the next dimension in life. Move into the future God has planned for you.

In grade school I was the only little colored girl in a class filled with predominately Caucasian children. I wore old, recycled clothes from the Goodwill and Salvation Army, my hair was kinky and short. I had a large forehead, a full nose, a little body and big feet—so I guess I looked a little peculiar to the other children.

I first started school with an impressionable mind full of life and no inhibitions about who I was, but after children in both elementary and middle school relentlessly teased me on my appearance, I was convinced of my inadequacies. My forehead was often the center of class jokes. My nickname in middle school was "Forehead." When the teasing first started, I brushed it off and didn't let it get to me and I never tried to defend myself because I was shy. But after facing the ridicule over the course of several years, I began internalizing the jokes and believed them to be true. My self-esteem was extremely low. I started wearing big, baggy clothes to hide my maturing body and long bangs to hide my big forehead, hoping to deter the children from talking about me. Break and lunch times were especially difficult as I often sat alone and isolated on a corner bench eating lunch in the cafeteria, trying to escape the vicious remarks of my classmates.

There were many nights I cried myself to sleep, distraught from the litany of verbal abuse my classmates spouted out like waterfalls. I hated going to school. I hated socializing with other kids outside of school. I hated everything and everyone and I especially hated myself. This self-contempt carried over into high school and even college. It wasn't until my early twenties that I was finally able to forgive my tormentors and move on from the past. Yet, even today, more than twenty years after leaving middle school, the scars from those painful moments remain.

So how has God used my suffering for good? I know throughout all of the hardships I've endured, God has kept me until now. He has provided me with unconditional love and turned a desolate life filled with self-pity and low self-esteem into one immersed in confidence and a sense of purpose. And because of my past, I have a heart for others who are dealing with similar circumstances and a desire to provide emotional support and encouragement.

The life story of Joseph in Genesis 37:1-50:26, provides a wonderful example of God working all things, even the painful ones, together for good. Joseph was one of Jacob's twelve sons. Joseph's ten older brothers believed he was their father's favorite and were jealous of him. This jealousy led to hatred and betrayal as they sold their brother as a slave and reported to their father that Joseph had been killed. Once sold into slavery, Joseph was taken to Egypt, where he served as a slave to Potiphar. Eventually Potiphar's wife falsely accused Joseph of attacking her, and Potiphar threw Joseph into prison, where he served several more years. Joseph could have become angry with God and hated all those around him for his unfair treatment. He could have viewed himself as a failure and lost all confidence. But he made a different choice. He chose to trust God. He chose to live with integrity and make the best of every circumstance. Consequently, throughout his years of hardship and suffering, we read that God was with him.

Eventually, God opened the door for Joseph to interpret Pharaoh's dream, and he was elevated to a position in Egypt second only to Pharaoh. When his brothers came to Egypt to seek food during a famine, Joseph reunited with them. His brothers feared Joseph would punish them for the evil they had done to him years before, but Joseph forgave them and helped them. You see, he knew God had a blueprint all along. He told his brothers, "But as for you, you meant evil against me; *but* God meant it for MY good, in order to bring it about as *it is* this day, to save many people alive," (Genesis 50:20 NKJV,). God will work things out for your good the same way he did for Joseph. Whatever you are going through, turn it over to the Lord and he will work it out.

God had a strategic plan for Joseph's life and although it was difficult to see, Joseph trusted and obeyed him, even during the darkest times. Eventually God brought good from all that happened. Joseph gained faith, wisdom, wealth and power, which he used for good. His people, God's chosen people, were saved from the famine and grew in great numbers in Egypt.

God also has a strategic plan for your life. He can turn your painful past into a joyous future, but it will require that you turn all your pain, hurt, and disappointments over to him. Then allow him to bless you—with love, joy, peace, prosperity and hope.

Although Satan's mission is to steal, kill, and destroy everything God created (John 10:10), the amazing reality is that despite Satan's attempts to manipulate the outcome of your life, God still finds ways to turn the situation around so all will work in your favor! Think back to some of the hardships and trials you've faced in life. Have you overcome any adversity? Have you survived situations you didn't think you would make it through? Are you still alive to tell your story? In case you didn't know, God has been watching over you!

You deserve the perfect peace God promises to those that keep their minds on him. Allow the joy of the Lord to be your strength. You don't have to live a life of misery or self-hatred. As powerful as God is, he loves you past all your flaws and mistakes. He loves you unconditionally. So if God can love you despite your imperfections, isn't it time to love yourself?

Let your self-criticism and complaints about the past end here. Be thankful for everything, including the challenges of the past, because all your experiences have made you into the person you are today. Trust and follow God and he will continue to work all things in your life together for good.

Affirmation: I accept the choices I've made in the past and will use them as life lessons to propel me to a brighter future. My past failures and disappointments do not define or predict my future success. I have a choice and I choose God's perfect and acceptable will for my life.

Action: Sometimes it's difficult to deal with painful memories, but healing comes from confronting these emotions. Stop suppressing your painful emotions and allow those feelings to surface. By letting go of the baggage, you will release the burdensome weight you've been carrying and come to a place of long overdue peace. For your journal entry today, reflect on your memories of hurt, neglect, pain, disappointment, violation, betrayal, disrespect, devastation, and all the emotions you have tried to suppress. Write about how these memories can and will positively affect your future. *Remember: God has your best interest in mind, so allow him to carry you through this process of reflection and healing.*

Food for thought: Some situations will require intervention from others. It may not be enough to just write out your feelings and pray over them. God is the ultimate healer of pain, but sometimes he works through others. Christ-centered support groups, counselors, psychologists and other trained professionals can help you appropriately deal with your pain. If necessary, use these resources to propel you to the future God has planned for you.

This poem was inspired after some reflection on my own past hurts. It's all right to cry, so let go if you need to...you'll feel better after the tears fall.

Yesterday the Tears Fell

Yesterday my tears fell
They fell long and they fell hard
They fell like a lagoon overflowing
and surged as a rushing river after a midday storm
Yesterday my tears fell
They fell heavy and they fell hard
As my soul, overwhelmed with sorrow, searched for an ounce
of relief
The sting of life's past overwhelms me
The pain of life's lessons have overshadowed my future
Staking its claim on my destiny
What was once an overflow of laughs and infectious smiles?
Is now extinct
Will I ever smile again?
How does my soul carry on?
When will my sorrow subside?
These tears that fall are weights far too burdensome to bear
My heart shatters from the disappointment of life's failed
promises
What now?
How do I stop these present tears from falling and my future
tears from consuming me?
Yesterday's tears seemed so far away, yet today they came and
took refuge in my heart and invited my present and future tears
along for the journey

When will my hurt—my pain—my grief fade away …
fade away…fade away?
When will yesterday's tears stop falling?
Yesterday my tears fell…and today my tears are falling
harder…perhaps tomorrow my tears will cease.

Bermesola M. Dyer, 2008

Take heed to yourselves. If your brother sins against you,
rebuke him;
and if he repents, forgive him. And if he sins against you seven
times in a day, and seven times in a day returns to you, saying,
"I repent," you shall forgive him.
Luke 17:3-4 (NKJV)

Day 6:
Forgive Others and
Forgive Yourself

Are you harboring resentment or holding on to anger from past hurts? Have you allowed these emotions to fester into a firearm or bombshell waiting to explode? The words of Christ found in today's scripture encourages us to forgive others when they have wronged us. Clinging to yesterday only stops us from moving on to our tomorrow.

Now that you have chosen to confront the past and deal with the painful memories, the next step is to make peace with your past and forgive anyone who has hurt you. Forgiveness is the only way you can move forward without the baggage of your past haunting you.

Wouldn't it be great if you could click your heels together and go back in time to undo past mistakes and disappointments? Unfortunately, no matter what you do, your past is there forever, never to be undone or changed. Your past may be filled with momentous occasions and blissful memories or it might encompass painful recollections and scars from frustrations and regrets. The benefit of what happened in the past is just that...it's the past. It's behind you. It's now time to find a way to let it go and move on with your life. If you are holding grudges or hard feelings towards people who have hurt you, it is time to let it go.

For many years I harbored resentment over broken relationships until I learned to accept the fact I couldn't force other people to remain connected to me or to treat me in the manner I desired to be treated. What I know now is that I can't control the actions of others, *but I can control how I allow them to affect me.*

I spent years hating the classmates who taunted me mercilessly until one Sunday when I heard a sermon on forgiveness. The message revealed how unforgiveness leads to resentment and bitterness and eats away at our soul. After hearing the sermon, I recognized that I was a bitter person who had been holding onto resentment and anger since middle school. This state of mind hindered me from being able to trust others. I wouldn't allow people to get close to me. After coming to this realization, I knew I needed to deal with my unresolved issues. At last I was finally able to exonerate the classmates I hadn't seen in more than twenty years. It took some time and was extremely difficult, but I was finally able to let the past go.

It is never too late to create a better future by choosing to forgive. Forgiveness will help you move past the despondent memories and begin a new chapter in your life. What happened in the past does not have to define your future. Perhaps your mother constantly put you down or your father mentally abused you. Maybe one of your teachers said you would never be successful or kids ridiculed you.

You don't have to be a victim of those past circumstances and the past doesn't have to define who you are or hinder the possibilities of your future. God's Word assures us that no weapon formed against a child of God will prosper (Isaiah 54:17). No matter how devastating your past may be, turn your circumstances over to God and allow him to heal those scars and set you free from the demons that haunt you.

Forgiveness doesn't suggest you have to welcome the person back into your life, become best friends or pretend the offense never happened. Forgiveness means you acknowledge what the person has done but refuse to allow the pain to continue holding you hostage. Release the bitterness and love the person with God's kind of love.

> But God demonstrates his own love for us in this:
> While we were still sinners, Christ died for us.
> Romans 5:8 (NIV)

Because Christ loved us enough to pay the price for our sins by suffering and dying on the cross, we can find forgiveness through him. Think about how loving and forgiving God is when we make mistakes and go against his will for our lives. He forgives us and casts our sins into a sea of forgetfulness, never to be remembered again (Micah 7:19; Psalm 103:12). If God can forgive us for the wrong we've done, surely we can forgive those who have wronged us.

> Make allowance for each other's faults, and forgive anyone who offends you. Remember, the Lord forgave you, so you must forgive others.
> Colossians 3:13 (NLT)

In some instances, the offender may not even realize he (or she) did something to offend you. While you are agonizing over the situation, the other person has moved on with his or her life clueless to what you have been going through. Sometimes all it takes is a phone call, a heart-to-heart talk or a thoughtful letter to work out the situation instead of dismissing relationships because of small disagreements. Perhaps you will not always agree, but working out the differences can bring you closer together and allow a friendship to reconnect and continue to grow.

If you have not forgiven someone who hurt you—whether 20 years ago or last week—take the first step today. Choose to forgive and let go. If possible—and appropriate—talk or write to the person expressing your decision to forgive. If personal contact is not possible or wise, you can find closure on your own. An act of forgiveness will facilitate the closure you need. You may want to raise your hands to God in prayer with your palms up as an act of giving the bitterness to him. Or you could write the offense and your feelings down and then ignite the letter into flames as an act of letting it go and giving it all to God.

Not only is it imperative to forgive others, it is also essential to forgive yourself. If you are holding something against yourself, receive the forgiveness of the Lord and let go of it. Jesus wants you to love not only him and others—he also wants you to love yourself.

> "Teacher, which is the most important commandment in the Law of Moses?" Jesus replied, "You must love the LORD your God with all your heart, all your soul, and all your mind. This is the first and greatest commandment. A second is equally important: Love your neighbor as yourself. The entire law and all the demands of the prophets are based on these two commandments."
>
> Matthew 22:36-40 (NLT)

Love your neighbor *as yourself*. One of the greatest ways you can love yourself is to forgive yourself. The first step to forgiveness is to seek God's forgiveness; if you've never done that before, you can elect to do so right now. We've all sinned but God sent his only son, Jesus, to pay the price for our sins. He offers forgiveness as a gift. We only have to believe that Jesus died for our sins. Ask for forgiveness, and choose to follow him.

> We are made right with God by placing our faith in Jesus Christ. And this is true for everyone who believes, no matter who we are. For everyone has sinned; we all fall short of God's glorious standard. Yet God, with undeserved kindness, declares that we are righteous. He did this through Christ Jesus when he freed us from the penalty for our sins. For God presented Jesus as the sacrifice for sin. People are made right with

God when they believe that Jesus sacrificed his life, shedding his blood.

Romans 3:22-25 (NLT)

When you received Jesus and his forgiveness, the sins of your past were erased. Although there may still be natural consequences from your previous wrongdoing, in God's eyes you are white as snow. Begin to see yourself through his eyes—cleansed and forgiven.

Even as Christians, we do things that displease God. But the Bible assures us that if we will confess our sin, he is faithful to forgive (1 John 1:9).

Because God has forgiven you, you can let go of the guilt and condemnation. Forgive yourself, forgive those who hurt you, and move on with your life. Satan will try to remind you of the wrongdoing and accuse you—but you can reject his accusations. He is a liar. Jesus has set you free!

Affirmation: Today I am moving past the hurts of my past and walking into a brighter bondage-free future.

Action: Write a letter to someone who hurt you. Genuinely let the offender know how you feel about what happened and how it has affected you. Tell the person that you are choosing to forgive. You can send the letter or just read it aloud to yourself. Afterward, you can burn it, bury it, shred it or throw it away. This will signify you are closing this chapter of your life and walking into the next phase without the baggage of your past. After writing a letter to the offender, write a letter to God asking for his strength to forgive and move on.

Sample Prayer:

Lord, I need your help to forgive the people who hurt me. I've tried so many times before to release the anger, bitterness, hate and resentment, but have been unsuccessful. I ask for your guidance and the strength to forgive others as well as myself. Please order my steps and restore my joy.

For everyone born of God overcomes the world. This is the victory that has overcome the world, even our faith.
1 John 5:4 (NIV)

Day 7:
A Victim of Circumstances ...Or an Overcomer

Yesterday you made a commitment to forgive others as well as yourself and to release the stronghold of your past. Today you face another choice. Will you allow yourself to be a victim of your circumstances—past and present—or will you overcome them and step forward to become all God has designed you to be?

Are you a child of God? Today's scripture tells us if you belong to him, you are an overcomer. How? By your faith in God's love for you and in his promises to you.

Your experiences, both good and bad, teach valuable lessons. Not only can you choose not to be a victim of hurts and negative experiences—but you can also choose to learn from them and grow.

When troubles come your way, consider it an opportunity for great joy. For you know that when your faith is tested, your endurance has a chance to grow. So let it grow, for when your endurance is fully developed, you will be perfect and complete, needing nothing.

James 1:2-4 (NLT)

The healing process will allow you to cultivate Godly fruits of the spirit such as patience, kindness and faithfulness from all you have endured. You're past is allowing you to grow into the positive and beautiful person God intended you to be.

For as he thinks in his heart, so is he.

Proverbs 23:7 (NKJV)

Keep in mind that transformation also comes by changing the way you think. Avoid using the past as a crutch or excuse to hinder you from reaching your goals. Put everything behind you that has stopped you from seeing yourself as God's gift to the world. Beautiful ...designed for a purpose...destined for greatness! The past is now behind you, and it's time to look forward to some of the best days of your life.

God's Word tells us that the transformation of our thoughts comes from hearing and understanding his Word.

Don't copy the behavior and customs of this world, but let God transform you into a new person by changing the way you think. Then you will learn to know God's will for you, which is good and pleasing and perfect.

Romans 12:2 (NLT)

As God transforms you from the inside out, you will become that beautiful person He created you to be. As you grow in him, you will exude confidence, charisma and joy. His love will flow through you and touch others.

Notice that none of the attributes mentioned above have anything to do with physical traits. The most significant part of who you are is your character. Beauty is not about how blue your eyes are, how long your hair is, or how much money you have in the bank. Those things come and go, but your character will last a lifetime.

Proverbs says this about the virtuous woman, "Charm is deceptive, and beauty is fleeting; but a woman who fears the LORD is to be praised," (Proverbs 31:30 NIV). Our outward appearance is constantly changing and fades away, but our inward beauty lasts a lifetime. Redirect your attention from external beauty to internal and spiritual beauty—that is what touches others and makes a positive contribution to the world.

It's your choice. Will you be a victim of your circumstances—or an overcomer?

Will you allow God to use all that has happened to you to help you grow into a beautiful woman of character?

Affirmation: God has blessed me with his strength and power. I am an overcomer! I will achieve my greatness. I will to step out in faith and believe in myself and the endless possibilities life has to offer.

Action: Today meditate on Proverbs 31 and begin to compare your character to the character of the virtuous woman described there. Which of those virtues are already in your life? Which need to be cultivated? What steps will you take to cultivate them?

Rejoice in the Lord always. Again I will say, rejoice!
Philippians 4:4 (NKJV)

Day 8:
Focus on the Positive

Do you see challenges as certain defeat...or opportunities for growth?

Do you focus on your weaknesses...or on your strengths?

Do you dwell on what you don't have...or give thanks for what you do have?

The Bible is full of scriptures that admonish the believer to be thankful for everything. No matter how bad our circumstances seem there is always something to be thankful for.

Sometimes we develop a pattern of destructive thinking in which pessimism becomes a way of life. Cynicism and skepticism can be the natural outflow from years of verbal, social and emotional abuse. If you have repeatedly endured painful circumstances, the negative thinking becomes a way of protecting yourself from potentially disappointing situations. Consequently, instead of hoping for the best you expect the worse. As a result of the constant negativity you can only see what you don't like about yourself and are blind to your strengths.

You may be filled with self-doubt and self-criticism, not knowing or believing God made you exactly the way he wanted you to be.

Perhaps you feel as though God could never love you. How could he care about someone like you? You don't understand that he loves you unconditionally. That he loved you enough to die for you.

Or maybe you feel as though he has let you down in some way; you've forgotten that every good and perfect gift comes from him. Just know that no matter what you are going through, the outcome will work out in your favor.

Perhaps some of these negative feelings have become second nature and are now a part of your daily thought process. Search deep within to recognize the habits you have formed and reprogram your thoughts to bring forth life and growth. The thoughts held captive in your mind are thoughts your heart will believe. What your heart believes, your mouth will speak. What your mouth speaks influences what happens in your life.

If you always focus on the negative, it's likely you will expect negative things to happen. This leads to life choices that will make your negative thinking become a reality. If you think you will always fail, you probably will. If you see yourself as unattractive, the inner glow that creates genuine beauty is concealed. Instead of continuing down a vicious cycle of negative thinking, begin to speak life into your situation. Work to see the positive in every circumstance instead of focusing on the negative.

Likewise, avoid individuals who bring negative energy into your life. It might require you to remove these people from your inner circle and perhaps even your outer circle. I'm not talking about loving family and friends who offer constructive criticism at times. We all need that kind of help. I'm referring to people who constantly put you down, make you feel inadequate or cause you to doubt your self-worth. In essence, people who see the world negatively.

It might be difficult and perhaps painful to let them go, and they may not understand. However, continuing to listen to people who speak negativity into your life will make it difficult, if not impossible, to change the way you think.

Avoid people who criticize you, talk about you or cause you to feel bad about who you are. Constantly hearing negative messages from others or yourself will perpetuate the vicious cycle of low self-esteem. It is counterproductive to have people in your life pulling you away from where you are trying to go.

Focus on the positive...

Focus on the blessings in your life...and thank God for them. "Give thanks to the LORD, for he is good; his love endures forever," (1 Chronicles 16:34 NIV).

Focus on the wonderful way God has created you. "Thank you for making me so wonderfully complex! Your workmanship is marvelous—how well I know it," (Psalm 139:14 NIV).

Focus on God's ever-present love for you. "And I am convinced that nothing can ever separate us from God's love. Neither death nor life, neither angels nor demons, neither our fears for today nor our worries about tomorrow—not even the powers of hell can separate us from God's love. No power in the sky above or in the earth below—indeed, nothing in all creation will ever be able to separate us from the love of God that is revealed in Christ Jesus our Lord," (Romans 8:38-39 NLT).

Focus on Christ's gift of eternal life. Receive his gift and follow him. "For God made Christ, who never sinned, to be the offering for our sin, so that we could be made right with God through Christ," (2 Corinthians 5:21 NLT).

Focus on God's plan for your life. "'For I know the plans I have for you,' declares the LORD, 'plans to prosper you and not to harm you, plans to give you hope and a future,'" (Jeremiah 29:11 NIV).

Focus on the strength you have in Christ. "I can do all things through Christ who strengthens me" (Philippians 4:13 NKJV).

With all of the bad that is going on in the world it's easy to let negative thinking consume you. As you begin to reflect on your life and the messages of hope, love and encouragement offered through the word of God, you will begin to realize that there truly is so much to be thankful for.

Affirmation: Today I choose to see my glass as overflowing. I am overflowing with the love of God. I will focus on the positive because I am more than a conqueror in every circumstance.

Action: Create your own affirmation and write it in your journal. Make a list of negative-thinking people with whom you need to spend less time. Write at least three scriptures that help you focus on the positive. Post them where you will see them often.

Therefore, in order to keep me from becoming conceited, I was given a thorn in my flesh, a messenger of Satan, to torment me. Three times I pleaded with the Lord to take it away from me. But he said to me, "My grace is sufficient for you, for my power is made perfect in weakness." Therefore I will boast all the more gladly about my weaknesses, so that Christ's power may rest on me. That is why, for Christ's sake, I delight in weaknesses, in insults, in hardships, in persecutions, in difficulties. For when I am weak, then I am strong.
2 Corinthians 12:7-10 (TNIV)

Day 9:
Acknowledge the Unchangeable

In the scripture above, the apostle Paul writes about a personal dilemma he faced, one so aggravating he compared it to a thorn in his side. Despite Paul's request on three different occasions to remove the thorn, the Lord said no. So Paul acknowledged the problem and turned it over to the Lord to deal with in whatever manner he saw fit. He accepted God's grace to be enough to see him through.

Like Paul, each of us has thorns that will not go away. These thorns may be doubt, feelings of inadequacy, insecurity, low self-esteem or physical flaws. We will now use the list you created on day three to lay all your concerns on the table and become completely exposed and vulnerable. Acknowledge that no matter what you do, some of these features are a part of who you are and cannot change.

God created us not only in his image but exactly the way he wanted us to be. He provided us with the gifts and qualities we need to accomplish our purpose. We all have attributes we wish in some manner were different, but they too are a part of God's masterful plan.

Some features like height, shoe size, race, skin color, gender and physique are unchangeable. Other characteristics like weight, hairstyle, insecurities, selfishness and stubbornness are changeable. (I recognize we are living in a time when plastic surgery can change just about anything, but to keep it simple, we will consider them unchangeable.)

Here are a few examples:

Changeable	Unchangeable
Weight	Height
Hair color	Shoe size
Hairstyle	Bone structure
Fashion and Style	Gender
Kindness	Race
Generosity	Genetic composition
Self-esteem	Complexion

Now it's your turn to make a list of features and characteristics you would like to change. Write them in the appropriate column below. As trivial as this exercise appears, it is a significant step in your healing process. Until you are able to come to a place of acceptance for the changeable and unchangeable, you will find it difficult to appreciate all life has to offer. Be honest and take your time making your list. (Use extra paper if you need to.)

Changeable	Unchangeable

Now that you created your list, reflect on the emotions that arise as you look over the list. Ask yourself the following questions:

1. Why do I want certain features to be different?

2. Why do I want to keep other features as they are?

3. Have my friends, family or the media influenced my desire to change who I am?

4. Do I trust their opinions? If not, why have I chosen to let their opinions define how I feel about myself?

Now create a list of qualities you like about your character and your physical appearance. I've created my personal list and placed it below as an example:

Character Attributes I Like	Physical Attributes I Like
Warm and bubbly personality	My electrifying smile
Patient	My straight teeth
Innovative	My slim figure
Insightful	My almond shaped eyes
Intelligent	My athletic abilities
Ambitious	My style of dress

Your turn . . .

Character Attributes I Like	Physical Attributes I Like

Affirmation: My body is beautiful. I have extraordinary features I will love and cherish.

Action: Devise a list of at least 10 of your best attributes. Write them in the space provided above.

The Serenity Prayer:
God, grant me the serenity to accept the things I cannot
change, courage to change the things I can, and the wisdom to
know the difference.
Reinhold Niebuhr, 1926

Day 10:
Accept the Unchangeable

After asking the Lord to remove the thorn in his side three times, the apostle Paul accepted it as a constant fixture in his life. He realized he needed to trust and depend on the Lord to carry him through (2 Corinthians 12:7-10). Yesterday we talked about acknowledging the unchangeable in our life. Today we will talk about the importance of accepting them.

Second Corinthians 12:7-10 and *The Serenity Prayer*, have helped me through many of life's obstacles. I recite them daily to remind myself I can only change what I can change and must depend on God's grace to see me through the rest. Worrying over things we have no control over is futile and unnecessary. I encourage you to pray over them and give them to God.

What we can accomplish is limited when we depend on our own strength and abilities, but we often lean on ourselves and forget we need God even when we are acting in areas of our strength. When we are acting in areas of weakness, we more readily recognize our need for God and lean on his unlimited power. Then we turn to him. That's what Paul learned. That's why he could say, "That is why, for Christ's sake, I delight in weaknesses, in insults, in hardships, in persecutions, in difficulties. For when I am weak, then I am strong," (2 Corinthians 12:10 TNIV).

As I have previously mentioned, throughout most of my childhood and adolescence, I hated everything about my body. One feature that I especially wanted to change was my complexion because it was uneven and filled with blemishes. I have stretch marks along my legs and backside, and the color of my upper body is three shades lighter than my lower body. I loathed wearing swimsuits because they revealed every flaw. I was ashamed to look at myself naked. It took years to finally love who I am physically.

The road to unconditional love requires you to accept all of who you are, especially the parts you don't like and cannot change. I struggled with this until I began to reflect on the unrestricted love God has shown me. He loves me even when I make mistakes and deliberately go against his will.

He loves me not only through his words, but he also shows me his love every day through what he does. I think about the doors God opens and the blessings I've received even when I didn't deserve them. The fact that I am still alive despite horrible decisions in my past proves that God is faithful and loving. I know I am not worthy of his kindness, but because of his unconditional love, he continues to provide for me and meets all of my needs.

I'll never be able to fully comprehend the extent of God's love for me, but being able to grasp just an inkling of his amazing love has caused my prayers to change. I ask him daily to teach me how to love myself the way he loves me. The love God has for me is unwavering. No matter what I do, how I look or how I act, his love is still there. God continues to love and provide for me and for each of us despite our imperfections. He has looked beyond all our faults and daily meets and supplies our needs. God has set the perfect example of what simple and true love is and how we should love ourselves and others. Whenever you get discouraged, just reflect on his love and use that to catapult yourself to a higher level of love for him, for others, and for yourself.

> We know how much God loves us, and we have put our trust in his love. God is love, and all who live in love live in God, and God lives in them. And as we live in God, our love grows more perfect.
>
> 1 John 4:16-17 (NLT)

Part of learning to love yourself is accepting the unchangeable things in your life, whether good or bad. This does not mean accepting any sin in your life. That requires confession and repentance. Nor does it mean accepting situations that you have the power to change. It does mean accepting the unchangeable, the way God created you and the situations over which you have no control. Yesterday you acknowledged some of those things. Today ask God to help you accept them.

Speak positive messages into your spirit so you begin to believe them. Write down scriptures that describe God's love for you, Christ's sacrifice for you, God's forgiveness and grace and God's perfect plan for you. Meditate on them day and night. Remember, God's grace is sufficient.

The goal for today is to accept yourself for being simply you. This includes everything you are, everything you are not and everything you will become.

Affirmation: I love me just as I am. I accept every unchangeable flaw and imperfection. God is molding me and equipping me for all he wants me to do. I love me for who I will be in the future and I love me for all I have endured in the past.

Action: For the duration of the thirty-day journey, incorporate this short prayer into your devotional time. *Lord, teach me how to love myself the way you love me. Teach me how to see myself the way you see me. Give me strength to accept all my unchangeable imperfections the way you have. Help me to be more like you.*

And I pray that your love will have deep roots. I pray that it will have a strong foundation. May you have power with all God's people to understand Christ's love. May you know how wide and long and high and deep it is. And may you know his love, even though it can't be known completely. Then you will be filled with everything God has for you.
Ephesians 3: 17-19 (NIRV)

Day 11:
Deserving of Love

I Am Deserving of Love

I am deserving of love,
I am deserving of a love that's drama free, pain free, and loves me unconditionally
I am worthy of a love that may not fully understand me but completely accepts me for the woman I am
This love accepts me for my imperfections, my want-to-be perfections,
My misdirection, with no exceptions;
It loves me for the love I have to offer.
I am deserving of a love that is constant and enduring
A love that follows me through the dark trenches of life
And carries me to the hills of hope, across the valleys of peace,

through clouds of joy, And pours into rivers of fulfillment.
I am worthy of a love that carries no baggage, no fear, no
deception, no doubt or anxiety
I am worthy of a love that is intertwined within the roots of my
soul
and consumes my innermost being.
This love encompasses the definition of my existence
and catapults me to higher altitudes of greatness
It digs deep past my insecurities, relates to my vulnerabilities and
offers strength during the fragile moments in life.
I am worthy of a love of my very own
I am deserving of a connection cemented in fidelity,
Clothed with integrity, inspired by passion and perseveres
through every obstacle.
I am filled with the beauty of your love. I am inspired by the
warmth of your love. I am me because of your love.
I am deserving of love
At...last...I have discovered love
For I have discovered you
I am worthy of love
I am worthy of you!
I am deserving of love.
Bermesola M. Dyer, 2008

When I first started writing "I Am Deserving of Love," I was writing about deserving love from another individual (a man). As I began to read and reread the poem, I realized the love I was looking for from someone else was a love I could and should be giving myself. I should be able to love myself unconditionally and accept me in every facet of my being. I should be able to love myself through every obstacle I face and every good and foolish decision I make. How could I ask someone else to give me this amazing kind of love if I was not even capable of giving it to myself?

Everything we desire to have in a loving and lasting relationship like attention, time, concern, commitment, compassion and affection are the same qualities we should be giving ourselves. Are we not worthy of our own love? If we can't give ourselves the love we need, why would someone else be able to reach this expectation? We each know ourselves better than anyone and we know what it takes to meet our needs. No matter how anyone else treats us, we deserve to receive love, especially the love we give ourselves.

You may wonder why you deserve love. It is not because of your virtues—or your faults, nor because of what you have or have not experienced. It's not because of your appearance, your abilities, wisdom or education. It's not because of your successes or failures. You deserve love because of God's grace, mercy and kindness. Romans 5:8 states, "but God demonstrates his own love for us in this: While we were still sinners, Christ died for us." John 15:13 declares, "Greater love has no one than this, that he lay down his life for his friends." God shows how much he loves us every day through the big and small gifts he continues to bless us with.

Not only do you deserve the love you give yourself and the love you receive from others, you can also embrace and appreciate the love God gives, which is another way to interpret this poem. Each day you wake from your sleep, God shows his love toward you. He shows his love to you through your loved ones, through the air you breathe, through the beauty of his earth, through the opportunities he gives you, through the strength, the peace, and the joy he provides. He shows his love to you through Jesus Christ. If you were the only person on the earth, Jesus would have died for your sins. He loves you that much. His love is unconditional and endless. He created love and is the ultimate expression of the kind of love you should have for others—and for yourself.

God loves you regardless of your circumstances. He loves you through your hurts and mends your heart when it is broken. God loves you even when you don't love yourself. He sees the beauty and potential in you even when you don't.

There were times I would stand in front of the mirror and cry because I hated the reflection staring back at me. I often cried out, "Lord, I can't stand this monster I'm looking at in the mirror. Why did you make me this way? Why couldn't you have given me a clearer complexion, smoother skin and longer, thicker hair? Why do I have to be so dark? Why do I have to be so skinny? Why can't I find someone to love me?"

After spending time in prayer, I heard the Lord whispering in my ear, "You are fearfully and wonderfully made. You were made in my image. You are beautiful and I love you just the way you are."

Sometimes all we need is a word from the Lord to carry us through the dark places in life. As you complete this thirty-day journey, continue to reflect on God's love. Think of how powerful he is. He created the earth and sky, the wind and rain, the grass and trees. All creation is his masterpiece. If the God of heaven and earth loved you enough to sacrifice his only son's life for you, surely you can learn to love yourself. You may never come to fully understand the height, the depth, or the total extent of the love God has for you, but just knowing that he loves you is more than enough!

Affirmation: I am deserving of love because God loves me. He loves me unconditionally. Because I am a child of God I am worthy of love.

Action: You may find this next action step a little challenging because it asks you to admire yourself in the simplest form of who you are. Stand in front of the mirror naked and unashamed. Affirm your beauty. Tell yourself how much you love every part of your body. Adore your silhouette, your love handles and the dimples in the most peculiar places. Appreciate your stretch marks, scars or gray hair. Don't be ashamed of your imperfections; your body tells a story of your life, your strength and your resilience.

In the same manner, extend all that you are to the Lord, exposing your strengths and weaknesses, your flaws, your dreams, your accomplishments, and your failures. His love comes without condition. Embrace his love, his forgiveness, his favor and his kindness.

Whatever a man sows, that he will also reap.
Galatians 6:7 (NKJV)

But the noble make noble plans, and by noble deeds they stand.
Isaiah 32:8 (NIV)

Commit to the Lord everything you do. Then your plans will succeed.
Proverbs 16:3 (NIRV)

Day 12: Devise a Plan and Follow Through

I f you carefully examine your past accomplishments and failures, they will reveal a strong correlation between the choices you've made, the actions you've taken, and the results obtained. The law of reciprocity suggests we reap what we sow in life. Nothing happens by chance.

Here's an example. Perhaps you're determined to lose ten pounds within the next two months. For this to happen, create a plan of action. Once the plan of action is created it must then be implemented—in essence…it's time to get to work! A sample plan might include working out thirty minutes a day four times a week, restricting meals to a certain number of calories each day, eating foods low in fat and sugar, getting at least seven hours of sleep, and drinking eight glasses of water each day. Sounds easy, right? Well, if you've ever tried to lose weight you know it can be quite the challenge unless you're willing to be consistent with the routine.

If you are uncommitted to the sacrifices required, unwilling to do the work, and unwilling to change your diet, it is safe to say that at the end of the two months, you will not reach your goal. Without action, goals and desires are impossible to achieve. You have to take the necessary steps to get the results you want.

In a previous chapter, you created a list of changeable and unchangeable traits. In this chapter, you will focus on the changeable traits and set a plan in place to change those things.

Ask God to guide you in setting your goals and making a plan to reach them. You might want to make changes in your physical appearance (lose weight), in your education (take a class or earn a degree), in your career (get a promotion, find a new job), in your character (be more patient, control your anger).

Write down these aspirations. Then prayerfully devise a plan. What action steps will you take to reach the goal? What is the timeline? Get started and then hold yourself accountable!

Motivation, commitment, and a relentless drive to succeed are key components in determining if you will reach your goal. Nothing comes easy. Your motivation will inspire you to initiate change. Your commitment will carry you through the process. Your relentless drive to succeed will enable you to achieve your goal. Each of us has been motivated to do something at some point in our lives, but the true test is staying motivated and committed until the task is complete. How long will you be able to stick to the routine to get the desired results? Staying committed is not easy, but you can do it! You can do all things because you've been empowered by the strength of God.

You are capable of greatness! God has blessed you with the tools you require to be successful in life. But you have to use the tools he has provided. The more you use them, the more skilled you become and the better the outcome. Making excuses about your past only keeps you from getting to the future you desire. No excuses allowed! It's time to take charge, take action and do what you've set out to do!

If you need tangible help to guide and encourage you, don't hesitate to seek out the resources available in your church or throughout the community. Do what's required to become successful. If reaching your goal requires a personal trainer to motivate you and keep you consistent with your work out and weight loss regimen, invest in a trainer. If you are struggling with your finances and need financial counseling to help bring you out of debt, invest in a financial counselor or take a class on finance management. If you are contemplating starting a business, invest in a business coach or consultant. Remember, if you continue doing the same things you've always done, you'll continue to get the same results you've always gotten. By taking one small step at a time eventually you will look back to find you've come a long way.

Affirmation: Today I will take a step toward reaching my goal. I will develop a plan of action and make a commitment to hold myself accountable. I will stick to the plan. I will not allow excuses to prevent me from achieving the goals. I will commit my plan to the Lord. Then I will succeed. I am determined and committed to reach my goals.

Action: Write out your action plan. When writing your action plan, be sure it is clear and precise with a start and end date. Here's an example to get you started:

Goal: Lose ten pounds in two months (put down the date)

Action Steps:

- Go to the gym for one hour on Monday, Wednesday and Thursday mornings.

- Run 30 minutes every Saturday afternoon.

- Keep a food diary and limit my calorie intake to 1200 daily.

- Get a physical.

- Eat only fruits and vegetables as snacks.

- Decrease desserts to two times a week.

- Weigh myself once a week.

- Find an online support group or a friend for accountability.

And we know that all things work together for good to those who
love God, to those who are the called according to His purpose.
Romans 8:28 (NKJV)

Blessed is the man that endureth temptation: for when he is
tried, he shall receive the crown of life, which the Lord hath
promised to them that love him.
James 1:12 (KJV)

Day 13:
Don't Give Up!

Life presents us with a spectrum of seasons, each bringing emotional highs and lows. Some days you may feel as if you are soaring among the clouds while looking at the world below. Other days you may feel as though the waves of a roaring sea are swallowing you. Are you in the midst of a tragedy or hardship? Perhaps you have lost a loved one or are healing from the remnants of a failed relationship. Maybe you are struggling financially and are unsure of how to make ends meet. Are you feeling dejected, isolated or alone? Whatever your story, I encourage you not to give up on yourself or on the goals you've set.

Sometimes it seems when we take one step forward, circumstances will push us four steps back. Whenever I am going through a difficult time, I find it helps to reflect on some of my better days. When I reflect over my life, I realize I am blessed with far more good days than bad ones, and my circumstances could be much worse. I remind myself that God didn't bring me this far to leave me. If I made it through the storms back then I can make it through the rain clouds now. God is watching over me and walking with me every step of the way.

No matter what you are experiencing, you can get through it. Meanwhile, rely on God's love to encourage you. Rely on his strength to keep you focused, and depend on his promises to sustain you. Don't give up!

God's love is enduring and relentless. When you are weak, he is strong. He promises he will never leave you nor forsake you. So be assured that his promise is as good as it gets. The Bible declares, "Heaven and earth will pass away, but his Word will stand forever,

(Luke 21:33)."

Forever is forever and God will never break his promise. When you are walking through a difficult place, know that he is with you. He promises to never leave you nor forsake you (Hebrews 13:5). Use these experiences to lean on him like never before. Use these challenges to increase your faith, for he is your rock and your salvation and in him you can trust.

Many Bible passages encourage the believer to rejoice in the Lord always. No matter what you are going through, thank him for his love, for being with you, for making all things possible. Even if you lose your job, lose your relationship, a loved one is sick, or you are struggling financially, never forget you serve a God who can do anything but fail. His Word decrees, "I have been young, and now I am old; yet have I not seen the righteous forsaken, nor his seed begging bread," (Psalm 37:25 KJV). God is faithful to his children. When one door closes, he will open another. Stand steadfast in God's promises to you.

God will always be there for you (Hebrews 13:5). He wants you to prosper, and he wants to bring you to an expected end (Jeremiah 29:11). His will is that you have an abundant life. As grim as your circumstances seem, you can be certain someone else is in a situation far worse than yours and wishes she could walk in your shoes. Even if you can't see it now, there is so much to be thankful for.

There were times I felt as if life wasn't worth living anymore. I felt as though I had nothing to offer anyone, not even myself. I frequently fantasized about death and contemplated driving off a cliff, slitting my wrist, or overdosing on pain medication. I was so unhappy in life. Between my low self-esteem and the inability to secure a meaningful relationship, I genuinely believed I had nothing to live for. I was dealing with so much pain and hurt that I mentally couldn't take the suffering. I lost weight, my hair fell out, I couldn't stand the sight of food and some days I barely had enough energy to get out of bed.

Learning to deal with broken relationships was especially difficult. I assumed that if the person I was dating no longer valued our relationship it meant that no one else would value being with me either. If I wasn't good enough for him, then I wasn't good enough for anyone. If I wasn't good enough for anyone, then what was the purpose of living? I felt unloved and presumed I had nothing to offer the world. Some may think I was overreacting, but for a young woman who had loved for the first time, dealing with abandonment and a broken heart was a devastating ordeal; I didn't know how to handle it.

Here I was just twenty-three years old and ready to end my life. I was depressed and cried until there were no tears left. I slept most of the day away. Thankfully, I never stopped praying and attending church services. Being in the house of God among the fellowship of other believers and hearing empowering messages gradually began to fill me with hope and encouragement, and I eventually chose not to give up on life. Despite all I was going through, this was the one place I felt safe. Week by week as I continued to pray and seek God's face, I regained strength. Eventually the broken pieces of my heart were mended.

I still had many questions. *What made him lose interest? Was it something I did? Was I no longer attractive to him? Did I not meet his expectations? Was there someone else? Was it because I wasn't giving enough of myself? Was it my hair? My weight? My clothes? What was it?* All of these questions chipped away at my self-esteem. I didn't realize it at the time, but I was more concerned about someone else's opinion of me than I was about my personal self-view.

It took nearly a year and countless hours of prayer for my heart to recover from that breakup. I relocated over

3000 miles across the country before I was finally able to completely accept closure. My self-esteem continued to improve. Several years later, my thoughts changed from wondering what I was doing wrong in my relationships to realizing that not every relationship was destined to last. I also came to understand there are always valuable lessons to learn about others and myself through difficult experiences.

Learning how to deal with a broken heart was a lesson I wasn't ready to learn but it was a lesson I needed to learn. The pain seemed unbearable and no amount of pain reliever or home remedy could alleviate the agony I felt inside. There was no way to escape the hurt. My only relief from the heartache came through time and prayer.

Ending a meaning relationship or losing a loved one is difficult, but it doesn't represent the end of your life. God didn't promise we would not experience sorrow or pain in our lives. What he did promise is that he wouldn't allow the tests and trials to overtake us. He said he would never put more on us than we could bear. This means nothing can overtake you, and better days will come. Yes, chapters do come to an end, but they lead to a new chapters beginning.

I think about the testimony of great people who defied the odds in dismal circumstances and reached success. One particular person who comes to mind is director, writer, actor and composer Tyler Perry. During interviews, Perry often talks about his challenging childhood, which included sexual molestation and homelessness. Tyler Perry was so full of shame and self-doubt he also contemplated suicide. What if he would have followed through on his plans to end his life? The plays, movies and positive messages he has used to reach millions of people would not exist. I'm grateful Mr. Perry decided to press through his pain. I'm thankful he decided to use his gift of writing as an avenue to heal his hurts. So many lives, including my own, have been encouraged and inspired by his messages.

It is difficult to predict what you can accomplish in life. However, if you choose to give up before you even start, how will you ever know what effect the lessons you learned from your story, testimony, struggles and triumphs will have on someone else's life? God placed you on earth for a strategic purpose. So as stated by Pastor Joel Osteen, "As long as you have breath, someone needs what you have!!" You have a mission to complete and a destiny to fulfill. Don't give up on your life.

No matter what you are going through, I encourage you to hold on to life. Hold on to your dreams. Believe in yourself and believe that God will help you walk this path. Don't give up. You can and will make it! Keep pressing forward. You are going to make it! God has not forgotten about you. He will bring you through every trial and every circumstance. Hasn't he brought you through difficult times before? Hold on to his promises. Put your hope in him. Don't give up!

Affirmation: I will not give up. With the help of God, I can and will survive every obstacle placed in my path. I am an overcomer. I will not give up on my dreams. I will not give up on life! I will not give up on myself!

Action: Write a list of the struggles you are facing. Ask these questions about each: *What good can I see even in this situation?*

How can God use this for his glory and my good?

How might I be able to minister to others once I overcome this struggle?

What lessons am I learning in the struggle?

In his grace, God has given us different gifts for doing certain things well.
Romans 12:6 (NLT)

That is why, for Christ's sake, I delight in weaknesses, in insults, in hardships, in persecutions, in difficulties. For when I am weak, then I am strong.
2 Corinthians 12:10 (NIV)

Day 14: Strengthen your Strengths

Several days ago, you listed some of your strengths and weaknesses. Today we will use your list to reflect on your strengths. Each of us has features and characteristics we consider our strong points. It could be a great smile, healthy hair, a good sense of humor, a great figure or a generous spirit. Maybe it's a charismatic personality, luminous skin, a kind heart, patience or intellect. No matter what your strengths are, cherish them. They are what make you unique. Use your strengths to reinforce the positive image you are striving to achieve.

Instead of focusing on your physical limitations and flaws, redirect your attention to the physical features you like most and work toward optimizing them. Let's say, for example, you have a beautiful smile that draws many compliments. This is an attribute you can use to enhance your outer beauty while reflecting your inner beauty. You can smile more, frown less and wear lip-gloss that accentuates that particular feature. If your hair is one of your favorite features, don't be afraid to let it shine for you. Wear that endearing hairstyle, rock that fabulous cut and work that vibrant color. Have fun being the best you can be. Augmenting your strengths will help boost your confidence.

Along with enhancing your physical features, you can also work towards developing your spiritual gifts. In 1 Corinthians 12, the apostle Paul talks about spiritual gifts and their importance to the body of Christ. What extraordinary set of gifts and talents has God given you? If you are unsure, answering questions like these may help.

What are you most passionate about doing?
What drives and motivates you?
What inspires you?
Can you sing or dance?
Are you athletic, charismatic or insightful?
Are you an organizer?
Do you write well?
Do you get excited about teaching the Word of God?
Are you patient, kind, generous, or loving?
Do you like working with children?
Are you good at explaining things?
Do you work well with numbers or money?
What are your gifts?

God has given you talents, gifts and strengths to enhance not only your life but also the lives of others. He has equipped you to fulfill his plan and purpose for your life. Take some time to discover your abilities and then fine-tune them. Don't let your talents and gifts go to waste.

In addition to answering questions similar to the ones above, ask people who know you well what they see as your strengths and passions. You might even want to complete a spiritual gift evaluation. You can find one online or ask your pastor if he recommends one. Several online resources are listed below to help you determine your areas of strength. Using these resources will assist you in identifying your gifts and talents. Reflect on the treasures you have and use them to draw others into the kingdom of God where they too can experience his unconditional love.

Once you recognize your strengths and gifts, seek God's will and ask him for guidance on how to use them to accomplish his purpose for your life. Strengthen your gifts by using them to serve others but be ever so careful to use your gifts in a manner that glorifies God and draws people closer to him as opposed to leading them further away. Many people have chosen to use their gifts in a manner that draws the masses down a slippery slope leading to sin and distance from God. Always remember that to whom much is given, much is required (Luke 12:48). God will hold us accountable for the impact we have on the lives of others whether for good or bad.

The world is waiting for you to realize your potential and use your gifts to make a difference. Don't keep your gifts to yourself. Share them with the world!

Affirmation: I have much to offer the world. My talents and gifts make me extraordinary and unique. My gifts are assets I use and do not waste. God has equipped me with these gifts to make a difference in this world, to fulfill his purpose for me. As he guides me, I will use them to make a difference in the lives of others.

Action: Study 1 Corinthians 12 and compose a list of your strengths, gifts and talents. What will you do to develop your gifts? The following table has three different categories and a few examples to help get you started. Consider joining a club or organization that provides opportunities for you to share your talent.

Additionally, these websites may help you answer questions regarding your spiritual gifts and talents.

1. http://www.kodachrome.org/spiritgift/
2. http://www.biblicalstudies.com/bstudy/spiritualgifts/ch08.htm
3. http://mintools.com/spiritual-gifts-test.htm

Character	Appearance	Skills/Gifts/Passions
Patience	Lips	Writing
Generosity	Legs	Dancing
Integrity	Eyes	Athletic

Your Turn . . .

Character	Appearance	Skills/Gifts/Passions

*They made me the keeper of the vineyards; but mine own
vineyard have I not kept.
Song of Solomon 1:6 (KJV)*

*If anyone does not provide for his relatives, and especially for
his immediate family, he has denied the faith and is worse than
an unbeliever.
1 Timothy 5:8 (NIV)*

Day 15:
Take Care of Your Needs

Have you become so preoccupied with helping others only to discover at the end of the day there is no time left for you? Perhaps you spend the core of your time caring for your children or aging parents, or meeting the demands of your career or church commitments. All of these responsibilities are important, and it's necessary to fulfill your obligations. But sometimes life gets out of balance—and these responsibilities begin to dominate your time and leave little time for you.

You may not intend to neglect yourself but sometimes life can move so fast that at the end of the day there is no time left to meet your own needs. Consequently, after years of helping others, it's not uncommon to find you've lost sight of your own dreams and hopes and forgotten who you are and what brings you fulfillment.

How many women do you know who are living their lives for their children? Between changing dirty diapers, taking kids to soccer games, gymnastics, football practice, helping with homework, cooking, cleaning, and going out for family time on the weekends, they have no life outside of parenting. When the children are grown and gone, mom's world comes crashing down because raising the children was all she knew. Should she have seen to her children's needs and done all she could for them? Of course! But the important word here is balance. *Balance, balance, balance!* Too much of one thing and not enough of another can be toxic!

Recently I had an opportunity to care for a woman in her mid-sixties who was hospitalized after suffering from a heart attack. While nursing her back to health I learned that her husband was also sick with cancer and she had been his primary care taker for the last year. She explained that because she was so concerned about his recovery, every minute of her day was devoted to taking care of him and his needs. Between doctor's appointments, physical therapy, preparing meals, giving medications, chemo-therapy, dressing changes and being his emotional support, by the of end day she was mentally exhausted and physically drained. She admitted to often skipping her own doctor's appointment or forgetting to take her own medications. This is the perfect illustration of what can happen when we become so immersed in meeting the needs of others that we neglect our own health and wellbeing.

The scripture above talks about being a keeper or caretaker of others but failing to take care of our own needs. Are you the woman who has spent her whole life trying to please or live for someone else? What happens when the other person is still not happy with the sacrifices you've made? What happens when that person is no longer in your life? Will you lose your identity and reason for living?

Take time out of the whirlwind of life to love, pamper and nurture yourself. Take time to seek out your purpose and your passions. Yes, others are depending on you, but how can you give them your best if you have nothing left to give? Taking time to rejuvenate and replenish yourself is essential not only for you, but also for those you care for.

It is our responsibility to be in good health, eat correctly and get the rest we need in order be a blessing to others. God requires that we present our bodies as living sacrifices to him, holy and acceptable in his sight (Romans 12:1). Would God be pleased with the lifestyle choices you are making? Would he be pleased with the amount of time you are spending on your temple? Are you neglecting it or taking it for granted? You only get one body. Refuel it with the proper rest; nourishment and exercise it needs; doing this will replenish you with the energy and strength needed to continue pouring into the lives of others.

Alongside the restoration of your body's health, how long has it been since you've refreshed your body's physical appearance? Is it time for a new hairstyle or a makeover? Are you still wearing the same old baggy sweats, oversized t-shirt and beat-up house slippers you've had for more than ten years? If you have ever watched a show on makeovers, you've seen how a new haircut, a little bit of makeup, and a new outfit can slice years off your appearance and boost your self-confidence.

Pampering yourself doesn't mean spending your entire paycheck on high-end spas and vacation packages. It simply means taking time out of each week to tune in to what your body needs. Meditate, pray, and be led by the Holy Spirit. Don't let the stress of your job, the pressure of bills, the care of children, your marriage or other responsibilities consume you.

Life is too short and the hours move too fast not to enjoy the precious moments. After years and years of giving yourself to others, one day you may wake up to realize that while you spent your entire life catering to everyone else, you lost your own identity in the process. Learning to balance and prioritize the responsibilities of life will allow you the time needed to invest in yourself and your mission.

Affirmation: Today and every day I will take time to refocus re-energize and renew my mind, body and soul. I will take care of my needs. I am deserving of love.

Action: Schedule at least ten minutes each day to meditate and pray, to reflect and re-center your thoughts and energy. Focus on becoming a balanced individual.

Therefore, rid yourselves of all malice and all deceit, hypocrisy, envy, and slander of every kind.
1 Peter 2:1 (NIV)

Dear friends, let us love one another, for love comes from God. Everyone who loves has been born of God and knows God. Whoever does not love does not know God, because God is love.
1 John 4:7–8 (NIV)

Day 16: Don't Be a Hater

There is no place for jealousy or envy in a child of God. As children of God he has called us to share his love and kindness with others. Yet all too often our hearts are filled with anger, hatred, envy, jealousy and bitterness, otherwise known as…"haterism."

The results of haterism lead to gossip, betrayal, backstabbing and deception. Haters are jealous of other people's success. They hate when others flourish, hate to see others shine, and hate to admit someone else is good at something. The results of haterism can cause the hater to undermine another individual's efforts and accomplishments to make them fail.

Haterism leads to the spreading of rumors. Christians sometimes do this under the guise of prayer requests. Genuine prayer requests are vital for unity and solidarity in the body of Christ. But when they are disguised gossip, they are detrimental to the cohesiveness and trust amongst the believers.

As women, we often scrutinize each other and criticize one another's shortcomings. We cast judgment on one another based solely on external appearances. Have you ever found yourself making remarks like these: *What is she wearing? Her outfit looks hideous! What possessed her to come out of the house wearing that? I look better than she does! She's ugly, she's fat and she has a big nose.* These statements are perfect examples of haterism.

Don't be a hater! No gossiping allowed! And don't get in the way of someone else's success. I have found that haterism often results from our own insecurities and low self-esteem. It takes little effort to look at another person, size her up and then judge her for what we see on the outside. But who are we to judge? And what right do we have to criticize or demean the efforts of someone else?

Think back to where you've come from. Are some of your struggles with low self-esteem the result of someone else's hate for you? Were there people in your life that talked about you, depreciated you or abused you verbally, physically, or mentally? Were people quick to judge you? And did that influence your feelings of inadequacy? If this is your story, how can you become the problem you are trying to escape? How can you treat someone else in the same malicious manner someone treated you? These destructive actions can be devastating and carry long-lasting emotional scars. God's word admonishes the believer to love our neighbors as we love ourselves (Matthew 19:19, NIV).

Your mission is to build up your self-confidence but it should not come at the expense of tearing someone else down in the process. God wants us to build them up too. Congratulate others on a job well done instead of being jealous of their accomplishments. I have found that complimenting someone else boosts my self-esteem. I feel empowered when I empower others.

> Be devoted to one another in love. Honor one another above yourselves.
> Romans 12:10 (NIV)

Jesus commanded us to treat others with love, respect and dignity. In turn, we can expect to receive the same treatment.

> "Do not judge, and you will not be judged. Do not condemn, and you will not be condemned. Forgive, and you will be forgiven."
> Luke 6:37 (NIV)

If you frequently find yourself judging others, ask yourself these questions: *What is the underlying reason I am critiquing someone else? Am I criticizing others because it makes me feel better about myself? Do I really feel good about myself after I have finished making someone else look bad?* If you have ever been the object of gossip or backbiting, you know what it feels like when others criticize you. Make a commitment to encourage others—and never to tear them down.

What about people who have hurt you? Perhaps even now they are judging you, gossiping about you. Jesus made the answer clear:

> "You have heard the law that says, 'Love your neighbor' and hate your enemy. But I say, love your enemies! Pray for those who persecute you!"
> Matthew 5:43-44 (NLT)

Do not allow your success to come at the expense of destroying someone else's sense of self-worth. There's no need for the crab-in-the-barrel mentality. That is when the crabs at the bottom of the barrel are constantly grabbing at the feet of the ones on top and pulling them back into the bucket so no one can escape. You are displaying this crab mentality when you constantly criticize others or are afraid to see them succeed. God created every individual differently, and our differences should be celebrated, not condemned. We were each born with our own purpose to fulfill. There are no mistakes or accidents with God's creation. Everything he makes is good! Therefore, no one has the right to judge others for their appearance or shortcomings.

Another way to show love and to improve your self-esteem is to help others in need or "pay it forward." For example, when my friend was about eight months pregnant, she decided to treat herself to lunch, but at the end of the meal, the waiter brought her a receipt marked "Paid in Full." Attached to the receipt was a note saying, "Please place the pregnant woman's meal on our tab but don't mention it until after we leave." As my friend revealed her story, I noticed a twinkle in her eyes and a glowing smile on her face. She talked about how wonderful it felt to have a stranger do something kind for her and how she wanted to pass the same kindness on to someone else. It's amazing how fulfilling it is to do a kind deed for others, especially when they aren't expecting it. I challenge you to try a random act of kindness and see how rewarding it feels.

> Don't look out only for your own interests, but take an interest in others, too.
>
> Philippians 2:4 (NLT)

Do you see signs of haterism in your life? Ask God to help you replace hurtful attitudes toward others with love, his kind of unconditional love. We are blessed to live in a country filled with endless opportunities for everyone to succeed. We can all do well in life without pushing others down on our way up. I've learned that it is easy to find fault in others, but the true challenge is finding and then appreciating the good in others. Anyone can gossip, but it takes a special person to compliment and love another. Encourage someone today, and celebrate with others when they succeed.

Affirmation: Today I celebrate our differences and appreciate our similarities. We are each beautiful in our own way. I applaud the success of others and want the best for them in life.

Action: For your action step today, do a random act of kindness. Compliment three people, treat someone to lunch, send a thank-you note or let someone know you appreciate them. Whatever you decide, make sure your actions uplift, encourage and inspire another to be the best person he or she can be.

Finally, brothers and sisters, whatever is true, whatever is noble, whatever is right, whatever is pure, whatever is lovely, whatever is admirable—if anything is excellent or praiseworthy—think about such things.
Philippians 4:8 (NIV)

Day 17: Watch What You Watch!

Our thoughts are a reflection of what we see and hear. Messages sent across the airwaves coax us to look, act, and walk in unison with popular culture. And if we don't look the part, we often feel less than adequate.

Low self-esteem could be a consequence of the stereotyped messages you've been watching every day. The media plays a significant role in the way we think and how we perceive ourselves. Just consider the billions of dollars advertisers spend on television, radio and print media with the goal of enticing us to buy their products. Have you ever watched a commercial about ice cream or doughnuts and suddenly developed a craving for junk food? If the advertising ploys were not successful, would companies continue to spend billions of dollars on useless ads? Their motives are calculated and they know exactly what they are doing. They are trying to convince us to buy into their products or the images they are selling. People are willing to spend money they can't afford on branded labels hoping to gain the clout those names carry.

Repeatedly hearing and seeing the same messages will lead to feelings of confusion and doubt about who you are or who you are supposed to be, especially if you don't fit into the "in" box. Perhaps there was a time in your life when you had a healthy sense of self-worth, but you are currently struggling with a deteriorating self-image. Do you feel that if you don't have the look of a supermodel or sport the image of America's rich and famous, you are not valued in our society? Did you at one point appreciate the dependability and comfort of the Toyota you worked so hard to pay off, but now believe that nothing less than a Mercedes Benz will do despite the high car note you would struggle to pay every month?

God fashioned each of us distinctly, equipped for his purpose for our life and our world. Sadly, so many people have sacrificed their God-given traits of individuality in an effort to achieve society's image of beauty and success. But these media-spouted images of "success" cause many of us to hate ourselves when we fail to achieve them.

After almost losing myself to the demons of my past and the negative images I allowed myself to entertain, I have finally come to understand how important it is to surround myself with positive influences. Now I am extremely selective of the people I associate with, the music I listen to, and the television shows and films I watch. I screen every image I allow to pass through my senses (whether through sight, hearing, touch, taste, or smell) and especially into my thoughts. I push out anything negative. I will not focus on messages that could jeopardize my positive self-image. I will not allow pop culture to infiltrate my mind with conflicting messages. Since I am what I think I am, and I will become what I say I will become. I must think on things that are good, lovely, praiseworthy and virtuous.

Once I understood the correlation between what I watched and how I thought, I cut some television shows out of my repertoire. Music videos were the hardest to let go. Videos set the pace for the current trends and styles—and, of course, there is the bonus of the gorgeous men on display. I deeply appreciate various genres of music. However, as I began to take a more critical look at some of the music videos, I noticed I was constantly seeing the same images: scantily dressed women dancing provocatively. They were being demoralized, and objectified as nothing more than human toys and prizes. Watching MTV, VH1 and BET was a favorite pastime. I was glued to the television screen everyday trying to emulate the latest video. Over time I noticed I was losing an important part of myself. I started feeling worthless and inadequate because I looked nothing like those women. If those were the women men wanted, where did that leave me? The video watching had to stop.

Although the media acts as a trailblazer, setting the stage for fashion and coaxing the masses to jump hastily on the bandwagon, its portrayal of beauty fails to appreciate our diversity. Popular culture reinforces the idea that anything outside the "beauty box" is unacceptable. If you are not a certain size or age or don't fit into a certain category, you are lead to feel like an outcast. It's no wonder so many young girls suffer from anorexia and bulimia. They try so hard to fit into a box that society defines as normal that they ruin their health and lose their identity in the process. The National Eating Disorders Association estimates that 7 to 10 million women and girls suffer from an eating disorder.

Are you trying to fit into a mold created by someone else's opinion? If the answer is yes, here's an opportunity to compose your own definition of beauty. Who is the media to tell you what beauty is? What qualifies popular culture to decide what is appealing? Beauty is a state of mind, not a state of body and is in the eye of the beholder. Be careful what you watch, listen to or read; they can destroy your self-image. Redirect your attention to God's Word and the messages it gives you about who you are in Christ. You are a direct and unique expression of God's creativity.

Affirmation: I will not entertain negative messages or allow the media to influence my self-image. I am a unique expression of God's creativity. God strategically designed me to be exactly who I am.

> I praise you because I am fearfully and wonderfully made; your works are wonderful, I know that full well
>
> Psalm 139:14 (NIV)

Action: Create a list of television shows you watch, magazines you read, and music you listen to. Decide whether they are helping or hurting your self-image. If they are damaging your self-image, cut them out of your life and ask God to lead you to positive media outlets.

> Don't copy the behavior and customs of this world, but let God transform you into a new person by changing the way you think. Then you will learn to know God's will for you, which is good and pleasing and perfect.
>
> Romans 12:1-2 (NLT)

Who can find a virtuous woman? For her price is far above rubies. The heart of her husband doth safely trust in her, so that he shall have no need of spoil. She will do him good and not evil all the days of her life. She seeketh wool, and flax, and worketh willingly with her hands. . . . She riseth also while it is yet night, and giveth meat to her household and a portion to her maidens. She considereth a field, and buyeth it: with the fruit of her hands she planteth a vineyard. She girdeth her loins with strength, and strengtheneth her arms. She perceiveth that her merchandise is good: her candle goeth not out by night.
Proverbs 31:10-13, 15-18 (KJV)
A Wife of Noble Character

Day 18: Define Your Beauty

What is beauty anyway? Do physical traits make one beautiful? Is it sex appeal? Personality or style of dress? What about height or weight? Bone structure or body physique? Perhaps it is the level of education. Is a college graduate more appealing than a high school drop out? Of course we can't forget about cash flow. Is a person with a six-figure income more attractive than someone making minimum wage? What makes a person beautiful?

The definition of beauty is abstract and encompasses countless variables. Regrettably, instead of looking at the person as a whole, our culture has the propensity to concentrate on physical appearances and rarely takes the time to know the individual on a more personal level before casting judgment. So often beauty is confined to a stringent set of shallow qualifications. But in reality, what one person finds appealing can be distasteful to someone else. The old saying, "One man's trash is another man's treasure," implies that just because someone doesn't appreciate your beauty doesn't mean you're not beautiful. Discovering your personal beauty must come from within.

I've raised many questions about the definition of beauty because I've learned there is no one right answer. Beauty is different for men and women, different for the young and old. There are also cultural and regional variations of beauty. One culture may believe women with hairy legs are appealing while another culture sees it as a turnoff. Some cultures like women with a little meat on their bones while others like women on the slender side.

The ways to define beauty are many, but the only definition that truly matters is the beauty you see within yourself. Seize the opportunity to discover and define your own beauty using God's Word as your guide. His Word offers an alternative to what the world sees as beautiful. God said you are fearfully and wonderfully made.

Physical beauty is only temporary. As we age, wrinkles begin to set in, hair starts to gray and thin and body aches and pains take over. What does last, however, are kindness, generosity, integrity, hard work ethic, and good heart. Godly character forms an inner beauty unlike anything the world can offer.

Proverbs 31 gives us a picture of this kind of beauty by describing the qualities of a virtuous woman. Her husband and children adore her, and her employees respect her. She takes pride in her appearance and clothes herself with the best of fine linen. She cares for her household and prepares them for difficult times. She's an intelligent business woman who has thought out her investments wisely. She is kind and generous to those in need. Most important, she loves and serves God. "Charm is deceptive, and beauty is fleeting; but a woman who fears the LORD is to be praised," (Proverbs 31:30 NIV).

Are you a virtuous woman? This is the kind of beauty that lasts. This is the kind of beauty that is truly genuine. This is God's definition of beauty.

If others are able to influence your definition of beauty, you are not walking in your own truth. Should the images that popular culture promotes as beauty be accepted over the image and identity God has proclaimed you to be through his word? Step outside the world's rigid box and compose your own definition—according to God's view.

A well-known quote by Robert Kiyosaki says: "What you think of me is none of my business, what is most important is what I think of myself." This statement reminds me that I cannot get caught up with other people's opinions of me. Someone will always have an opinion and it may not be what I want to hear. What I've got to focus on is what I think of myself. Do I love myself unconditionally? What about you? Are you molding yourself to fit into popular culture? Think back to your childhood days and the peer pressure you faced. Did you always follow the crowd or did you dare to be an individual? And what about today? Are you seeking our culture's brand of beauty or God's brand of beauty which starts on the inside and works its way outward?

Many of us are trying to achieve someone else's definition of beauty and forget to appreciate the beauty we already possess. It's time for each of us to exemplify beauty in our own unique God-given way.

Affirmation: Beauty is in the eye of the beholder. When I look at myself, I see a breathtaking woman filled with splendor, beauty and purpose. I see a child of God, fearfully and wonderfully made in his image. I am everything God says I am. I am the head and not the tail. I am above and not beneath. I am blessed coming in and blessed going out. From this day forth, I choose to portray my own definition of beauty. I will not allow the images others present to hinder me from seeing the beauty within myself.

Action: Define what beauty is to you. Does your definition align with God's? In the areas where it is out of alignment, ask the Lord to conform your image to agree to his.

I can do all things through Christ who strengthens me.
Philippians 4:13 (NKJV)

So if the Son sets you free, you will be free indeed.
John 8:36 (NIV)

I praise you because I am fearfully and wonderfully made; your works are wonderful, I know that full well.
Psalm 139:14 (NIV)

Day 19:
Break Free Independently

Do you often look to other people or material things for validation and acceptance? If so, you could be setting yourself up for big disappointments. Friends and family—even well-meaning ones—will sometimes let you down. They may not be around when you need them and at other times they just don't know how to help. And in some instances they completely turn their backs on you during your time of need.

Money, material things, popularity and other earthly solutions might help you feel better about yourself for a while. But they are only temporary fixes. Today's topic deals with breaking free of low self-esteem without the crutches we often use to make ourselves feel better. These crutches can be the trust we put in money, other people or material items.

When you realize other people and things do not always make you feel good about yourself, how do you respond? How do you handle feelings of abandonment, hurt, anger, mistrust, disappointment and betrayal? People commonly seek refuge from the pain in alcohol, drugs, promiscuous lifestyles and other unhealthy behaviors. But these are not lasting solutions. When the high from the pipe has come down, the buzz from the booze has faded, and the one-night stand is gone, you're left alone to deal with the sadness, the bitterness, the regrets, and the continuing insecurity.

During your hours of loneliness, you must find the strength to persevere and a way to encourage yourself with hope and a determination to overcome. All this comes from only one source: God.

One of my favorite inspirational stories in the Bible depicts the steps David took on the road to becoming the king of Israel. Throughout much of 1 Samuel, King Saul was chasing the soon-to-be great King David. Saul despised David because he knew he would take his place on the throne. Saul tried everything he could to destroy David, but there was a covering of God's protection over David's life. No matter how Saul tried to kill David, he was unsuccessful. Throughout most of 1 Samuel chapters 16 through 31, David was trying to escape Saul's relentless pursuit. As an outcast of Israel, David was homeless and hungry. He was forced to hide in caves and live among the enemies of Israel for protection.

At one point, Saul's soldiers surrounded David and his army on every side, and it seemed as if death was inevitable. David's men were fearful and without hope. The odds were stacked against him. Nevertheless, even when everything he could see spelled disaster; David found a way to encourage himself. He trusted God. He believed God would bring him through that situation, and God did just that. The Lord allowed the Philistines (Israel's enemy) to attack Israel, forcing King Saul to stop chasing David and fight Israel's attackers. This allowed David and his men the opportunity to escape to safety.

How did David encourage himself? He placed his hope and trust in God. He wrote songs and poems, he prayed, he cried, he danced; he called out to God and told him what was on his heart. The book of Psalms shares many of David's prayers and songs. David endured insurmountable hardship during that time in his life, but he didn't lose hope—and God saw him through. David didn't place his faith in the strength of his warriors. He didn't look for victory through powerful weapons. And he didn't trust in his own intelligence. Although he used all of these things, he knew that real victory would only come from God. He trusted God's love for him—and he trusted God's plan. Despite everything he went through, David did eventually become king of Israel. Through his faith in God and God's love for him, he was able to make it through those difficult times.

God protects his children from the hands of the enemy. There is no need to agonize over how your situation will work out. God has already told you what the result will be. If you trust Jesus and follow him, all things will work together for your good. Meanwhile, your responsibility is to break free of your low self-esteem. This means breaking free from depending on the clothes, the car, the friends, the money, the career, the drugs or the men to validate who you are. You cannot hide behind people or material items. It doesn't matter how much money you make, or how much education you have or don't have, or what kind of car you drive. Material items do not determine your status in life. When the clothes come off and the money is spent, you will still have to deal with who you are.

And who are you? You are God's creation. You are magnificent. He loves you unconditionally. Jesus died on the cross for you. You are extraordinary indeed!

In the past, during my darkest times, my crutch was shopping. Whenever I was feeling down, I would head to the mall for some "shopping therapy." I couldn't wait to buy more "stuff" because I thought that more "stuff" would make me feel good. I spent much of my hard-earned money on items I couldn't afford, with the hope that the "stuff" I had would make me feel better about myself and the situation I was dealing with. I shopped to escape my problems. I shopped to hide the pain. I shopped to avoid the real issues. I didn't understand that what I was really running from was myself. Shopping was nothing more than a distraction preventing me from dealing with the real problem.

I believed that buying more "stuff" would add value to my life. I shopped above and beyond my means because I thought I needed to buy designer clothes, wear the latest fashions, and drive a fancy car to make myself feel accepted. I assumed if I could impress others by looking good on the outside, I would feel better about myself on the inside. But what I discovered was that no amount of clothes, money, status or recognition from others would help me deal with not liking who I was. After I finished shopping and spent all the money and had all of the "stuff," I was still empty, broken and searching for love.

What crutches are you using to escape the pain in an effort to feel better about yourself? Examine some of your habits and practices. Ask if what you are doing in your spare time is the result of a low self-image. If it is, work to change those habits and begin focusing on Jesus' love for you. You are a child of the King!

Keep in mind there may be people in your life who do not want to see you succeed. Not everyone has your best interests at heart. Pray to discern the hearts of men and rely only on God and his strength to help you break free from a lifetime of pain and hurt. Depend on the constant and enduring love of God to carry you through. He whom the Son sets free is free indeed (John 8:36)!

Affirmation: I am magnificently made and worthy of love because God created me and loves me without condition. The Word of God determines my self-worth, not my material possessions or the people in my life.

Action: Create your own method to encourage yourself in the Lord. Find a passage of Scripture you will use for strength during difficult times. Listen to empowering messages and inspirational songs, speak affirmations and read God's Word daily. I've listed a few of my favorite scriptures below to help get you started.

- The Lord is my shepherd; I shall not want. Psalm 23:1 (KJV)

- I can do all things through Christ who strengthens me. Philippians 4:13 (NKJV)

- For I know the thoughts that I think toward you, saith the LORD, thoughts of peace, and not of evil, to give you an expected end. Jeremiah 29:11 (KJV)

- God blesses those who patiently endure testing and temptation. Afterward they will receive the crown of life that God has promised to those who love him. James 1:12 (NLT)

- The LORD is my strength and my shield; my heart trusted in him, and I am helped: therefore my heart greatly rejoiceth; and with my song will I praise him. Psalm 28:7 (KJV)

Here is a poem I wrote while dealing with my own self-esteem issues.

If I Had Created Me

If I had created me, my parents would have been rich.
I would have had two sisters and two brothers
and attended all private schools.
If I had created me, I would have been six feet tall,
a supermodel with long flowing hair,
flawless golden skin, almond shaped eyes,
size 7 shoe, and a 36-24-34 hourglass figure.
If I had created me, I would have had the face of Halle Berry,
the body of Serena Williams, the voice of Whitney Houston,
the sex appeal of Beyonce, a backside like J-Lo, the charm of
Julia Roberts, and a bank account like Oprah Winfrey.
Instead, I have four brothers and am a product of the public
school system.
I stand five foot seven, with chocolate brown skin, a
complexion full of imperfections, and feet so big I need shoes
special ordered.
My hair is quite kinky and shoulder length at best
and my body…well…where do I even begin?
I have some love handles and stretch marks on my butt,
my teeth are nowhere near straight, and my nose is wider than I
prefer.
And my breasts…well, they're probably dime size at best.
If I had created me, I would have been a completely different
person…
I would have been a unique image of someone else.
Instead…
My Creator knew who I would be even before I was conceived.
He created me in his image and gave me a heart filled with love.
He transformed my mind and showed me how to view my

body and love it without condition despite its flaws.
He gave me a voice to speak words of encouragement to those
in despair.
My hands serve those in need and demonstrate kindness to
those who may be suffering.
He replaced my sadness with joy and gave me peace of mind.
My Creator opened my eyes, changed my perspective, and
revealed the importance of being a person of integrity and
intellect.
I'm now glad God made me just as I am.
Who better to be than me?
I am beautiful and wonderfully made in His image.
Bermesola M, Dyer, 2007

But you are a chosen race, a royal priesthood, a holy nation, a people for his own possession, that you may proclaim the excellencies of him who called you out of darkness into his marvelous light.
1 Peter 2:9 (ESV)

Day 20:
Know What You Stand For

As a young girl, I worked tirelessly to mold myself into the image and likeness of the other children. I didn't like being different and wanted to be someone my schoolmates would accept. Because I suffered with low self-esteem, I often did things I knew were wrong because I wanted the other children to like me. I desperately sought their approval because I believed their acceptance would help me find my own acceptance.

On the contrary, I soon learned that my efforts to have others validate me only led to disappointment. I found myself constantly getting into trouble for following behind the other children and engaging in counterproductive activities. When it came time for the group of children to confess wrong doing, they singled me out as the scapegoat. Too shy to stand up for myself, I took the penalty.

This pattern continued into adulthood. My low self-esteem caused me to make bad decisions in relationships. I often stayed in unhealthy relationships because of my desperate need for someone to love me. Sometimes the people who claimed to love me blatantly disrespected and deliberately lied to me. Still, despite the pain and hurt I suffered, I stayed in these harmful relationships because I didn't want to be alone...and I didn't believe I deserved anything better.

My outlook on relationships didn't change until I began to understand who I was in Christ. Because I am a child of God, I am an heir to the throne and kingdom of God. I am part of a chosen generation, a royal priesthood, and a holy nation that has been set apart from the world (see today's scripture).

As believers, we are children of royalty. As children of God, we should settle for nothing less than God's best for us?

You are worthy of God's best. As an heir to the throne of God, you are an invaluable asset to his kingdom. Because you belong to him, you are priceless. You have the right to the abundant life God has designed for you. "Don't give your pearls to the pigs," my mother used to say when I was growing up. (I later learned this was her paraphrase of Matthew 7:6—"Don't waste what is holy on people who are unholy. Don't throw your pearls to pigs! They will trample the pearls, then turn and attack you.") She reminded me that people won't always appreciate my worth but I must stand my ground by not letting others take advantage of me.

You are one step closer to reaching your goal when you can base the standard for who you are on God's Word, not people's opinions. Take a stand for what you believe in. Jesus loved you so much he died on the cross to pay the price for your sins. When you receive him as Lord, you are clothed in his righteousness. See yourself through God's eyes. Live to please him, not other people. Refuse to live in a manner that contradicts your values and faith or forces you to compromise your integrity.

It is a common occurrence to hear messages in music and media outlets that refer to women as garden tools (h***) or female dogs (b****), but we do not have to accept this degradation. We must stand up as women of God, created by him for a Godly purpose. We must set the standard for ourselves and how we will allow men and even other women to treat us. We must set the tone for what we will and will not tolerate.

Are you subjecting yourself to late night rendezvous and one-night stands because you don't want to be alone? Are you engaging in an adulterous love affair hoping one day he'll leave his wife for you? Are you being mistreated or abused because you're afraid to leave and don't believe you can make it on your own? Are you wearing skimpy, seductive clothing to get men's attention? Are you listening to music that denigrates women or portrays us negatively?

We must be mindful of how we present ourselves to others because the manner in which we dress, the decisions we make, and the company we keep are our testament to the world about who we are and what we stand for. We must demand respect because we know we are heirs to the throne of God. He designed and equipped us to make a difference in this world and to accomplish great things for him.

Some people allow others to mistreat them because they feel they don't deserve better. I know this firsthand. I was that person. While growing up, I allowed people to walk all over me, talk about me, mistreat me—and still claimed them as friends because I didn't know who I was or what I stood for. The life lesson I later learned is when people can't give me the respect I deserve, they shouldn't be in my personal space. If the people in your life can't respect your decisions or are constantly criticizing you, do you really want them in your life?

Developing a healthy self-image requires a backbone that doesn't bend when the pressure rises. I've heard countless stories of women who desperately sought the attention of others and found themselves stuck in abusive relationships they couldn't escape because they didn't believe they were worthy of receiving anything better. Don't let this happen to you!

By staying grounded in the Word of God, you will be empowered to see yourself as God does. But remember, distractions and temptations are all around you trying to divert your attention. If you shift your focus away from God's standards, do not be surprised if you find yourself engulfed in what everyone else is doing and lose sight of who you are. Don't be afraid to eliminate the outside noise and extraneous messages. The only messages you can afford to hear right now are the reassuring ones coming from the Word of God.

Always remember: Stand for something or you will fall for anything!

Do You Know Who You Are?

...you are a chosen race, a royal priesthood, a holy nation, a people for his own possession, that you may proclaim the excellencies of him who called you out of darkness into his marvelous light.

1 Peter 2:9 (ESV)

Affirmation: I am a woman with insurmountable value and worth. My standards are set high and based on God's Word. I will only permit people who respect me and honor my values into my personal space.

Action: Make a list of the requirements you have and what you will and will not tolerate in your relationships, work environment and life in general. Set boundaries and standards for yourself and then make a commitment that no matter what happens, no matter how difficult life gets, there is no backing away from those standards.

A few examples:

1. I will not allow anyone to abuse me physically, mentally, or emotionally.

2. I will not stay in a relationship that is not nurturing or one that makes me feel bad about myself.

3. I will not continue a relationship with anyone who belittles me.

So all of us who have had that veil removed can see and reflect the
glory of the Lord. And the Lord—who is the Spirit—makes us more and
more like him as we are changed into his glorious image.
2 Corinthians 3:18 (NLT)

But the LORD said to Samuel, "Do not consider his appearance or his height, for I have rejected him. The LORD does not look at the things people look at. People look at the outward appearance, but the LORD looks at the heart."
1 Samuel 16:7 (NIV)

Day 21:
Stay Out of the Mirror

The mirror can be our worst enemy or our best friend. It tells no lies and exposes all truths. Sometimes it's difficult to look in the mirror and acknowledge our flaws without hating what we see. If you have put on a little weight, it will let you know. If there is a huge zit on your nose, the mirror will be sure to point it out. If you have spinach stuck between your teeth, the mirror, unlike some friends, will let you know that too. In the mirror you see who you really are—or do you?

For years I used the mirror to scrutinize my imperfections. I searched out every flaw and then condemned myself because of them. I discovered it is mind over matter when it comes to the mirror. The mirror only reinforces what you already believe. If you don't think you're beautiful before you look in the mirror, you will not see the beauty you possess during or after your time in the mirror.

If you stand in front of the mirror and look for every flaw you have, you will make yourself miserable. If this is your experience, just stay out of the mirror! Stop the self-criticism, stop the self-hatred and stop looking for things to complain about. Stop hating yourself. Just stop it all!

Limiting your mirror time means only staying in its reflection long enough to get dressed and to make sure everything is in order. When you are done, get out of there! There's no time to pick and fuss over every blemish, zit, gray hair, skin roll, stretch mark and wrinkle on your body. You will literally drive yourself to a place of discontentment.

Are you leaving the mirror never to return? No. Leave it only until you are able to appreciate the truly important attributes of who you are. God's Word is the true mirror because it reflects those things that are important to God. Those things that make you the person you are. Your attitude. Your character. Your walk with God. "People look at the outward appearance, but the LORD looks at the heart (1 Samuel 16:7)."

Ask God to help you see yourself through his mirror. Use his mirror to guide you, to develop a way of life more pleasing to him—one that will make a difference in the lives of others.

Obey the Word of God. If you hear only and do not act, you are only fooling yourself. Anyone who hears the Word of God and does not obey is like a man looking at his face in a mirror. After he sees himself and goes away, he forgets what he looks like. But the one who keeps looking into God's perfect Law and does not forget it will do what it says and be happy as he does it. God's Word makes men free.

James 1:22-25 (NLV)

Remember the mirror of God's Word reflects your inner beauty and his glory. Once you accept this, return to the mirror on your wall. Look into it and see the reflection of a virtuous woman of God, designed by him to fulfill a unique purpose.

Affirmation: I am a woman of virtue. I see beauty and splendor when I behold the image in the mirror.

Action: Place scriptural affirmation cards around your mirror so everywhere you look, you see positive messages. Recite them aloud every time you view your reflection on the wall.

I have fought a good fight. I have finished the work I was to do.
I have kept the faith.
2 Timothy 4:7 (NLV)

None of us are responsible for our birth. Our responsibility is
the use we make of life.
—Joshua Henry Jones

Day 22:
Leave Your Mark

God has gifted each of us with a specific amount of time to live out our lives. The time we spend here on earth will define our lives after we leave. What mark will you leave? What will others remember about you?

Are you making an impact in someone else's life? Are you changing the world for the better? Are you making a difference? What are you doing with your gifts and talents?

Some of us can sing, others can write, while others have the gift to teach or speak. Some have a gift for leading, or encouraging, or giving. Whatever your gifts are, you have a responsibility to find them, develop them and use them to make a difference in the lives of others.

Several years ago, I found myself swimming in a pool of self-pity. I was angry that my life wasn't where I intended it to be. My master plan was to marry by the time I was 26. I wanted to have the perfect job by age 27 and be earning a generous income by the time I was 28. I also wanted to be in the process of starting my own business.

At the age of 29, I was devastated that I had not reached these goals. I felt like such a failure and wanted to put my life on hold until at least one dream came true: my dream of getting married. I was wallowing in such self-pity. I could not see that there was more to life than dating, working and spending money.

My "aha" moment came after reading a passage in *Essence* magazine by Susan L. Taylor, the magazine's former editor-in-chief. She wrote of "the dash" between our birth and death. While we are living the dash, we have choices to make about how we will live our lives. Will we use this time to shape our world and serve God's highest calling for us or squander away the precious moments and opportunities we have? When we reach the end of the dash, it's too late.

That article helped me to recognize my time on earth is limited. I am responsible for making the most of it while I'm here. I want God to be pleased with what I have accomplished during my life. My desire is to hear him say, "Well done, my good and faithful servant." I want to know that I made a difference and helped change someone else's life.

Are you focusing on what you haven't done? On the negative circumstances in your life? On waiting for marriage or the perfect job before you start to live life to the fullest? You are running out of time! It's time to get past whatever is holding you back. Let go of your insecurities and start living the life you were meant to live. Don't wait until your life is almost over to finally accept yourself. It's time to leave your mark!

If you haven't discovered your purpose for living, what are you waiting for? You can spend your entire life wandering around aimlessly without finding your reason for being on this earth. What is your purpose? Your visions, dreams and aspirations for life? What mission did God place you on earth to accomplish? Your life has God-given meaning. Walking in your purpose is what life is all about.

Someone else is depending on your experiences, your struggles and the wisdom you've gained along life's path. There is more to life than looking good and spending money. When your life has ended, what will the Lord say when you stand before him? Will he say well done, or will he say you wasted your life away?

The longer it takes you to get past the low self-esteem, the longer it will take to realize your purpose and begin walking in the fullness of your calling. Each of us has unlimited potential. We can do all things through Christ. Dr. Myles Munroe stated in his journal, "The graveyard is the richest place on earth. Across the globe lay the remains of people who never reached their full potential or allowed their dreams and accomplishments to come true."

Don't let your gifts go to the grave! Use them to bless the people around you. Don't let your insecurities stop you from being the person God has called you to be. Don't let your hang-ups hinder you from reaching your full potential.

What will you do to make a difference? How will you leave your mark?

Affirmation: I am on earth for a specific mission and purpose. I am the only one who can walk in the life specifically designed for me. God has given me the tools I need to fulfill my purpose. I will complete my mission. I will leave my mark!

Action: Prayerfully create your own mission statement. A mission statement will help you remain focused on what God placed you on earth to do. Without one, it's easy to walk aimlessly through life without any direction or purpose. Write your mission statement down on paper and put it in a place where you can read it daily. To help you get started, here is my personal mission statement.

My Mission

My mission in life is to be salt and light in this world filled with darkness.

I will live with integrity and compassion, and possess a servant's generous spirit. I will have a positive influence on the people I come across throughout my life's journey. I will devote my efforts to the God I serve and walk in an upright and blameless manner. I will treat all people equally and love unconditionally. I will strive for excellence and not mediocrity. I am the head and not the tail. I will demonstrate beauty and grace in everything I do. I was born to make a difference in the lives of others, to bring blessings, words of wisdom, psalms of encouragement and a message of hope. I am destined for greatness. This is my vision and it will become my reality.

But I press on to possess that perfection for which Christ Jesus first possessed me. No, dear brothers and sisters, I have not achieved it, but I focus on this one thing: Forgetting the past and looking forward to what lies ahead, I press on to reach the end of the race and receive the heavenly prize for which God, through Christ Jesus, is calling us.
Philippians 3:12-14 (NLT)

So teach us to number our days, that we may gain a heart of wisdom.
Psalm 90:12 (NKJV,)

Day 23:
No Excuses!

Have you thought about writing a song or book, creating your own clothing line, choreographing a dance routine, or starting your own business? Well, what are you waiting for? Are you putting it off because you don't have the money, education or connections?

When I was in high school, I often said: "When I get older I'm going to do something great with my life. I'm going to be a lawyer or a doctor." When I reached my twenties, I continued making great claims—for the future: "When I get older I'm going to write my first book, get a doctorate, start my own business... I'm going to do something great with my life."

By the time I was in my late twenties, I began to reflect on my life and realized that for fifteen years I continued to say I was *going* to do something great with my life. That is until someone asked me what I was waiting for. When would older come and what's wrong with right now? The life lesson I learned was that I didn't have to wait until I had millions of dollars like Oprah or Bill Gates to make a difference in someone's life. In fact making a difference doesn't require any money at all—it only requires a desire and a willingness to serve.

So even if you are young, gifted and broke, don't let that be an excuse. The apostle Paul mentored Timothy, who eventually became a pastor. In his instructions to Timothy, Paul said this:

> Don't let anyone think less of you because you are young. Be an example to all believers in what you say, in the way you live, in your love, your faith and your purity.
>
> 1 Timothy 4:12 (NLT)

Acts of kindness can make a difference in someone's life. A friendly smile or compliment, a ride home, an offer to help someone in need, a thoughtful card, a word of encouragement, or a prayer for someone in distress will show that you care. We don't have to wait until we're older or wealthier to accomplish what God calls us to do. The world needs us now. Who's to say that we'll be around to get old anyway?

From the time we were born, God equipped each of us with the tools, gifts, and talents needed to contribute to the growth of humanity. The key is to put our gifts to use. Each of us must decide how and if we will use them.

Have you noticed a problem? Are you waiting for someone else to fix it? What's stopping you from doing it? Look at all the people who have made a difference in the world—teachers, nurses, doctors, civil rights activists, writers, and entertainers. What do they have that you don't? Yes, they are talented, but so are you.

And then some people who make the biggest difference in the world are unsung heroes: Godly parents and grandparents, mentors, and encouragers. These are people who take every opportunity to use the gifts God gives them.

Are you sharing your gifts with the world? Time is fleeting and there are no guarantees you will be around tomorrow to do the work you have the opportunity to do today. Will God be pleased with what you have done with your time? There is no time for excuses. Every day we get closer to completing our journey on earth. It's time to get to work! Walk in your calling. Reach your dreams. Fulfill your purpose.

Are you ready? Will you choose to enhance, improve and refine your gifts? Will you use them? Or will they just sit on a shelf, collecting dust?

Will you make excuses—or will you make a difference?

Affirmation: I have a gift to share with the world. I have an assignment given to me by God that only I can complete. I can change the lives of other people. I was born to make a difference. I am destined for greatness!

Action: It's your time to step out and make a difference. Set a deadline to finish your book, get your degree, start your business. Follow your dreams. Develop an action plan to fulfill a long-term goal.

Examples:

1. I will complete my book in one year.

2. I will earn my bachelor's/master's/doctoral degree in three years.

3. I will begin today to write a business plan and finish it in three month.

4. I will start my business in two years.

Death and life are in the power of the tongue: and they that love it shall eat the fruit thereof.
Proverbs 18:21 (KJV)

Set a guard over my mouth, LORD; keep watch over the door of my lips.
Psalm 141:3 (NIV)

The words of the reckless pierce like swords, but the tongue of the wise brings healing.
Proverbs 22:18 (NIV)

Day 24:
Your Words Have Power

Together we've explored how outside factors can affect our personal perceptions. We've talked about the lasting impressions the media, popular culture, relationships, friends, and family members have left on our minds.

Now that you have grasped how negative words from others—and sometimes even yourself—can lead to the development of a poor self-image, today's life lesson is to understand how speaking positively from God's Word can help you build a positive self-image. Refuse to allow destructive talk to have any power in your life. Turn off the noise that contradicts everything you are trying to become. It's time to tune in to what God wants you to be—and to speak words of affirmation from his Word.

The Word of God repeatedly proclaims there is power in your words. Revisit today's scripture, "Death and life are in the power of the tongue." Death and life and are in the power of the words you say!

God has equipped you with the tools you need to succeed, one of them being the words that you speak. As you walk out his plan for your life, choose words of faith, hope, persistence and patience. Speak words that affirm. You can do anything you set your mind to with the help of God. Your words are your choice. The words you choose will foster visions of victory or visions of failure. Your words will lead to the fulfillment of your mission or frustration from falling short.

The Bible says we overcome by the words of our testimony (Revelation 12:11). The words you speak influence your future. Someone may have spoken a negative word over your life when you were younger. They said you'd never amount to anything. They said you were worthless and good for nothing. Don't let destructive words from other people determine your destiny. You can reverse those negative words. You have the authority to speak God's Word into your own life. His words over your life will ultimately stand. Recite what the Word of God says. Let your own words, backed by the Word of God, take you to your destiny.

Today use your words to show how God helped you overcome adversity. Thank him for making you a stronger, wiser and a better person. Leave a legacy for generations to come and reclaim the power the enemy tried to steal from you through the words of others. *You will determine your success in life and it begins with the words you speak.*

Affirmation: As I trust in God's Word and follow him, my destiny is in the power of my words. I speak words of favor, success and unconditional love into my life.

Action: During your devotional time, search for at least five scriptures that will empower you when you are going through a challenging time. Write them out and recite them aloud during your prayer time.

Here are some possibilities to get you started.

No weapon formed against you shall prosper, And every tongue *which* rises against you in judgment You shall condemn.

Isaiah 54:17 (NKJV)

Submit yourselves therefore to God. Resist the devil, and he will flee from you.

James 4:7 (ESV)

The thief comes only to steal and kill and destroy. I came that they may have life and have it abundantly.

John 10:10 (ESV)

Have I not commanded you? Be strong and courageous. Do not be frightened, and do not be dismayed, for the Lord your God is with you wherever you go."

Joshua 1:9 (ESV)

And my God will supply every need of yours according to his riches in glory in Christ Jesus.

Philippians 4:19 (ESV)

And the Lord will make you the head and not the tail, and you shall only go up and not down, if you obey the commandments of the Lord your God, which I command you today, being careful to do them.

Deuteronomy 28:13 (ESV)

Commit your actions to the LORD, and your plans will succeed.
Proverbs 16:3 (NLT)

Trust in the LORD with all your heart; do not depend on your own understanding. Seek his will in all you do, and he will show you which path to take. Don't be impressed with your own wisdom. Instead, fear the LORD and turn away from evil. Then you will have healing for your body and strength for your bones. Honor the LORD with your wealth and with the best part of everything you produce. Then he will fill your barns with grain, and your vats will overflow with good wine.
Proverbs 3:5-10 (NLT)

For we are God's handiwork, created in Christ Jesus to do good works, which God prepared in advance for us to do.
Ephesians 2:10 (NIV)

Day 25:
Don't Be So Hard on Yourself!

In previous chapters, we discussed the importance of setting goals and actively pursuing them. But sometimes we can expect too much of ourselves. Have you ever set unrealistic goals and refused to be satisfied with nothing less than perfection. It's no wonder so many people suffer from stress and anxiety and are on the cusp of a nervous breakdown. We must find balance in the expectations we place.

Although we should strive for excellence, perfection is impossible. There are no perfect people in the world, and when we place the bar higher than is obtainable, we set ourselves up for disappointment and failure.

Are you pressuring yourself to excel, succeed, be flawless or meet the unrealistic expectations of others? Do you have impossible expectations of yourself that have led to disappointment and pain? Is well done ever good enough? Are you asking others to meet these impossible expectations?

There's nothing wrong with wanting to excel, but when your ambition starts to interfere with your health and peace of mind, it's time to slow down and reevaluate whether the expectations are unrealistic. Are you having sleepless nights and stressful days? Are you suffering from high blood pressure, stomach ulcers or migraine headaches? Is it difficult to find time to eat right, work out, or otherwise take care of yourself? Are you neglecting quality time with the Lord? With your family? Or yourself? If your answer is yes to any of these questions, you may be expecting perfection and striving too hard.

How many people have you known who worked hard to reach a level of excellence and then suffered from a heart attack, stroke or nervous breakdown because of the pressure they placed on themselves? There is a fine balance between greatness and going overboard.

Consider this: What is the motivation behind the goals you've set? Are you trying to meet someone else's expectations? Impress others? Compete with others?

Don't be so hard on yourself! You don't have to win

people's approval, set a record or reach perfection to make yourself important. It's God's approval we need—and he already knows we are not perfect. That's why he sent his only son, Jesus, to pay the penalty for all of our imperfections. When we receive Jesus, we become fully acceptable to God.

If you are living a life filled with stress, anxiety and unreasonable expectations, reflect on the underlying motivation. Are you pushing yourself beyond human limits? Slow down. Take time to regroup. You are wonderful because God created you. You are important because God loves you. You are acceptable because Jesus died for you. You can do all things—in Christ's strength, not your own.

Set challenging goals—but not impossible ones. Be sure they line up with God's plan for your life. He has prepared you and he is with you. You can succeed!

Strive to do all things well and to obey God in all you do. But when you fail, don't beat yourself up about falling short. Learn from your mistakes and move on. Don't condemn yourself. God knew we would stumble along the way, and he provided a solution. His word says:

> If we confess our sins, He is faithful and just to forgive us *our* sins and to cleanse us from all unrighteousness.
>
> 1 John 1:9 (NKJV)

Affirmation: I accept myself for the woman I am and for the woman I am becoming.

I am a work in progress but I am fully acceptable because of what Christ did for me. When I fall, I will not condemn myself but will ask for forgiveness, learn from my mistakes, and move on.

Action: Here's another—do something nice for yourself day. Buy yourself some flowers. Treat yourself to dinner, a movie or a play. Do it by yourself and enjoy your own company.

As iron sharpens iron, so a friend sharpens a friend.
Proverbs 27:17 (NLT)

Remember that mentor leadership is all about serving. Jesus said, "For even the Son of Man came not to be served but to serve others and to give his life as a ransom for many."
Mark 10:45 (NLT)

Day 26:
Find and Be a Mentor &
Role Model

We can all benefit from having mentors and role models in our lives. Mentors and role models provide inspiration and motivation to reach our full potential. Mentors push us to be the best we can be while offering words of wisdom and guidance along life's path. They set examples, offer constructive criticism and show us how to overcome obstacles that seem impossible. A mentor can be just about anyone: parent, friend, teacher, counselor or pastor. No matter who the person is, he or she contributes to our lives by empowering and motivating us to excel by refining and using our gifts and talents. Role models are people we emulate or admire.

They may not always be someone we know on a personal level but as a result of their contributions to the world they inspire us to overcome the hurdles that hinder us from reaching our greatness.

My parents have been my number one role models when it comes to hard work. They started from humble beginnings with little money or resources. Because of their faith in God and their determination to provide for their family, they have been able to accumulate assets reaching over a million dollars. Through their example, I have learned the importance of investing, sacrificing and delayed gratification. As a young girl they instilled in me the importance of perseverance and determination even when things were not going my way. Now, years later I can look back over my life and see how those qualities have been instrumental in my success and growth.

Role models who have encouraged me in the arenas of beauty and business are supermodels Tyra Banks and Iman. Both Tyra and Iman have set an excellent precedent for black women. Not only are these women breathtakingly beautiful with unique features, prominent foreheads, and deeper shades of black, but they are also intelligent entrepreneurs and successful businesswomen. I write "prominent foreheads" because this was a part of my body that I had the most difficulty accepting when I was young. The other children often teased me about my forehead being larger than normal so seeing beauty icons with similar facial features enabled me to love a part of me I once despised.

Iman has inspired a love for my dark complexion. Before she came along, there were few black supermodels with darker skin tones. Seeing her in magazines, on billboards, and on television fostered an appreciation for my dark skin. Tyra Banks was often teased because of her prominent forehead and slender build when she was younger. Now she is a beauty icon, loved and adored by men and women around the world.

These two women encouraged me through their grace and beauty to believe that I was a beautiful woman too, despite not having the traditional "pretty girl" look (whatever that is). I am still sultry, sassy, fly and fabulous! Find a mentor and/or role model to inspire you especially if their strengths are in places where you are struggling. Your mentor can help propel you to the place you need to be and your role model can inspire you to look past your insecurities.

Alongside the benefits of having a mentor, I've learned that I empower myself by empowering someone else. Not only is it important to have a mentor—it's also essential that we mentor someone else. How valuable are the truths you have learned on your journey through life? Can someone else benefit from your experience and insight? Can hearing how you worked through your challenges and struggles encourage someone else? We all have a testimony or a story to tell of how we made it through our trials and tribulations. Even if you're still in transition and haven't reached the place you'd like to be, you have a story to tell.

Someone out there needs your encouragement, your wisdom and your shoulder to lean on. They need you to help pull them up when they are down. They need you to help them see their beauty and potential when they can't see it within themselves. Someone needs to know your story and what you have gone through and how you've survived. You have a testimony to tell, a heart to inspire, and a soul to lead to Christ. Don't keep what you've learned to yourself; use your wisdom to educate someone else.

One of the most memorable and fulfilling times in my life was during the summer of 1998, when I was 22. I finally decided to share my story on a retreat provided through the organization "All That Women and Girls." The title of the retreat was, "Loving the Woman in the Mirror." When I first heard the subject matter I knew I was in trouble. For more than ten years I struggled with self-hatred, but that year was the most difficult as I had contemplated suicide on three different occasions. I was despondent, depressed and hated the reflection I saw in the mirror. From the outside looking in, one could not easily sense the inner turmoil I struggled with because I worked hard to camouflage the pain, but on the inside, I was secretly falling apart.

Many of the conference seminars required the participants to carry a pocket mirror around. Throughout various points in the sessions, the organizers instructed the participants to stare into the mirror and recite aloud what we loved about the image we saw. As simple as this task may seem, I found it extremely difficult. The hatred, hurt, and anger bottled up inside me made it hard for me to see my value.

At the end of the conference, I had an opportunity to give my testimony. I shared my story with the group of women and girls and talked about my long battle with self-hatred. The sixty or so young girls and their mothers wept as they listened to my story. At the end of the testimony I encouraged the girls not to put each other down because they would never fully understand the impact their words could have on someone else's life.

Here I was twenty-two years old and still dealing with the demons of my childhood. I still heard the voices of the past: "Big Forehead, Blackie, Crispy Cream, Burnt Piece of Toast, Olive Oil and Skinny Minnie!" I shared how those names haunted me for over a decade. And even now, as I write this in my thirties and reflect on those trying times of my childhood it touches a special place in my heart.

A life-changing moment transpired after I shared my story with the group. Many of the school age girls stood up and began to tell their stories. They spoke of their pain and hurts, their disappointments, their feelings of rejection and how they too struggled with low self-esteem. They thanked me for sharing my story and for inspiring them to treat other girls with love and respect. Some even made a commitment to stop bullying other girls and many vowed to love themselves unconditionally.

I must admit I had some reservations about revealing my inner secrets to a group of people I didn't know. But afterwards, revealing my true thoughts lifted a huge weight. It was even more empowering to hear the girls share their testimonies. Knowing I had influenced their lives positively enabled me to find the strength to take the next step, which was to find my own self-acceptance. My journey to self-acceptance began by giving my testimony that day and seeing the impact it made on the lives of others. I want to encourage you to build someone else up because as you build him or her up, you will be uplifted too.

Affirmation: I graciously accept the words of wisdom and encouragement from mentors and role models who have walked this road before me. I offer words of wisdom and encouragement as a role model and mentor to those that come behind me.

Action: Ask God to send a mentor into your life. Ask him to lead you to a person you can mentor.

Consider becoming part of mentoring organizations like these:

1. Boys & Girls Clubs of America (www.bgca.org)

2. Big Brothers Big Sisters (www.bbbs.org)

3. National CARES Mentoring Movement (www.caresmentoring.com)

4. The Mentoring Center (www.mentor.org)

5. Christian Association of Youth Mentoring (www.caym.org)

6. Christian Mentors (www.christianmentors.org)

But we glory in tribulations also: knowing that tribulation worketh patience; And patience, experience; and experience, hope: And hope maketh not ashamed; because the love of God is shed abroad in our hearts by the Holy Ghost which is given unto us.
Romans 5:3-5 (KJV)

I consider that our present sufferings are not worth comparing with the glory that will be revealed in us.
Romans 8:18 (NIV)

"I have told you all this so that you may have peace in me. Here on earth you will have many trials and sorrows. But take heart, because I have overcome the world."
(Words of Jesus)
John 16:33 (NLT)

Day 27:
It's Not Your Fault

I wrote today's devotional especially for the person whose traumatic life experience has affected her in such a way her world will never be the same. I dedicate today's devotion to victims of rape, child abuse, domestic violence, accident or injury, terminal illness, broken heart or physical disability. I'm speaking to anyone who has suffered an experience that has made it impossible to believe there is light at the end of the tunnel. If this is your story, I want to impress upon your heart a spirit of hope and optimism and encourage you to break through the pain of the past to a better tomorrow.

Life will bring challenges beyond your control and then force you to try to solve the problem with minimal resources. These challenges may seem unreasonable and unfair and steal a portion of your strength daily. I think about the woman in a physically or verbally abusive relationship who has repeatedly tried to escape the situation but somehow ends up back in the hands of the abuser. I think about the woman diagnosed with a terminal illness and given six months to live—she isn't ready to die yet, but her appointed time is nearing. Or what about the woman who was burned over sixty percent of her body after a house fire? When she looks in the mirror, she sees a monster even she is afraid to behold. Then there is the woman who can't move by herself because she is paralyzed from the neck down after her car spun off the road, hitting a tree. She now relies on the benevolence of others for her very survival.

Sometimes life doesn't make sense, and we can find no comforting answers to our questions. When strength leaves and you have nothing left to hold on to, the love of God and his promises will always be there. Cling to the promises in God's Word. He promises he'll never leave you by yourself. No matter what you are going through, I want to offer you hope that can only be found in Christ. Even if friends and family disappear when you need them the most, God is still there.

When the Lord Jesus Christ came down from heaven to live on earth, he knew he would only be with us for a short time. His mission was to save us from our sin and lead us out of a path of destruction and into eternal life. During his time here, he performed many miracles, touched thousands of lives and formed a new covenant between man and God. Despite all he did for the world, those he loved still rejected, ostracized, ridiculed and betrayed him. As his life on earth rapidly approached its end, he faced the ultimate form of rejection. He was put to death for showing us how to love and have compassion. At the end of his life, he died an extremely painful and agonizing death. Many scriptures speak of his suffering but also speak of the comfort he left behind for those who love him, "For the more we suffer for Christ, the more God will shower us with his comfort through Christ," (2 Corinthians 1:5 NLT).

God did not promise this life would come without pain. If Jesus suffered, we know that we too will suffer. You can find comfort, however, in knowing he has promised to leave his peace with you. No matter how grave the situation seems, God is still a healer, a deliverer and a way maker. He can make the impossible happen. God is still walking with you every step of the way! Whether you are lying in a hospital bed with minutes to live, sitting in a wheelchair with no feeling in your legs, recovering in a burn unit, or nursing wounds from the assault of an abusive relationship, God is still with you! You are still his child and he cares about you. Do not be discouraged. You are not alone! The Lord loves you dearly and is waiting with open arms to exchange your pain for his peace.

When you have nothing left to hold on to, nothing left to live for, and nothing left to believe in, you can still believe in God's Word. And you can find comfort and hope there. I pray you find rest in him. There will come a day when your suffering will be no more. If you believe in the Lord Jesus Christ and you are a child of God, you will one day rest in glory with him. There will be no more suffering, no more pain, no more sorrow—only joy unspeakable!

I am praying for your strength through these challenging times. I've listed several scriptures below that have given me encouragement during my times of need. I pray they encourage you too.

For the mountains shall depart and the hills be removed, But My kindness shall not depart from you, nor shall My covenant of peace be removed," Says the LORD, who has mercy on you.

Isaiah 54:10 (NKJV)

You will keep *him* in perfect peace *whose* mind is stayed *on You*, because he trusts in you.

Isaiah 26:3 (NKJV)

Peace I leave with you; my peace I give you. I do not give to you as the world gives. Do not let your hearts be troubled and do not be afraid.

John 14:27 (NIV)

And the peace of God, which transcends all understanding, will guard your hearts and your minds in Christ Jesus.

Philippians 4:7 (NIV)

The LORD himself goes before you and will be with you; he will never leave you nor forsake you. Do not be afraid; do not be discouraged.

Deuteronomy 31:8 (NIV)

Lo, I am with you always, even unto the end of the world. Amen.

Matthew 28:20 (KJV)

Be careful for nothing; but in everything by prayer and supplication with thanksgiving let your requests be made known unto God. And the peace of God, which passeth all understanding, shall keep your hearts and minds through Christ Jesus.

Philippians 4:6-7 (KJV)

Weeping may endure for a night, but joy cometh in the morning.

Psalm 30:5 (KJV)

Affirmation: When I have stood the test, I will come out as pure gold. God said he'd never put more on me than I can bear. God alone is my hope and refuge he will never leave me.

Action: Reflect on these difficult times. What are you learning about yourself, life, and other people? How have you matured or grown as a person? What new insight or wisdom have you gained from this experience? Can you offer a newfound truth or word of encouragement for someone else who is going through something similar? Share your story with someone else.

Test or Challenge	How you have grown because of your test

*Blessed is the man who perseveres under trial, because when he
has stood the test, he will receive the crown of life that God has
promised to those who love him.*
James 1:12 (NIV)

*We can rejoice, too, when we run into problems and trials, for
we know that they help us develop endurance. And endurance
develops strength of character, and character strengthens our
confident hope of salvation. And this hope will not lead to
disappointment. For we know how dearly God loves us, because
he has given us the Holy Spirit to fill our hearts with his love.*
Romans 5:3-5 (NLT)

*And I am certain that God, who began the good work within
you, will continue his work until it is finally finished on the day
when Christ Jesus returns.*
Philippians 1:6 (NLT)

Day 28:
Getting Past the Ugly...
Look How Far You've Come!

I t's been a long and challenging journey. You've made it past your insecurities, low self-esteem and distorted body image. You are beginning to let go of what other people think about you. You've endured the painful memories of your past, accepted the difficult truths of your present and learned to live for your future. Actually, you are probably still working on all of these issues, but look how far you've come!

You are truly a force to be reckoned with. You have made it this far. The key now is to never return to where you've come from and continue moving forward.

Do you remember how you got here? If so, you will know how to avoid going back to where you were. Here are a few things to avoid:

1. **Criticism from other people**: When someone is continually putting you down, you will eventually internalize what they are saying and believe it to be true. There's nothing wrong with constructive criticism, but criticism that is not constructive is destructive. Stay away from it and from people who never have anything good to say.

2. **Negative thinking and debilitating thoughts:** Thinking negatively about your circumstances can never bring positive results. Remember you are what you think. Always think positively and have an optimistic outlook on your situation. You'll be amazed to see what a difference a thought makes.

Reflect on this:

Whatever is true, whatever is noble, whatever is right, whatever is pure, whatever is lovely, whatever is admirable—if anything is excellent or praiseworthy—think about such things. Whatever you have learned or received or heard from me, or seen in me—put it into practice. And the God of peace will be with you.

Philippians 4:8-9 (NIV)

3. **Abusive relationships**: Abusive relationships are difficult to escape. The pattern of abuse cycles like a merry-go-round. At the end of the ride, it is difficult to get off because it's time to start the ride again. Ask the Lord for help. Ask him for the strength, resources and support you need to remove yourself from that relationship. Abusive relationships will continue to tear away at your self-esteem. These relationships can even cost you your life.

4. **Misleading media messages**: The media's messages often contradict the Word of God and can strip you of your God given identity. Be vigilant and mindful of what you watch and hear. Allow only messages in line with God's Word to penetrate your thoughts. You will eventually reap the harvest from what you sow into your life. If trash is going in, then trash will come out. If you keep God's Word hidden in your heart; that truth will be manifested in your life.

Whatever it took to *get you out* of your negative patterns is the same thing it's going to take to *keep you out*. Replace the negative experiences with positive ones. Fill your life with the truth of God's Word so you won't fall victim to the deceptive messages of the world.

Affirmation: I am getting closer to my goal. I will focus on what I want to achieve. I will not give up no matter how difficult my circumstances seem. God is my rock, and he will guide me through.

Action: Look back over your journal entries from the past few weeks. Celebrate successes and examine areas where you may need to improve. What you are learning is a process that should continue after this time of renewal.

Below is a list of resources for Domestic Violence:

- *http://www.nrcdv.org/ National Resource Center on Domestic Violence*

- *http://www.the hotline.org*

- *National Domestic Violence Hotline: 1-800-799-SAFE (7233)*

For once you were full of darkness, but now you have light from the Lord. So live as people of light! For this light within you produces only what is good and right and true.
Ephesians 5:8-9 (NLT)

But the Holy Spirit produces this kind of fruit in our lives: love, joy, peace, patience, kindness, goodness, faithfulness, gentleness and self-control.
Galatians 5:22-23 (NLT)

Day 29:
You Are Your Greatest Asset
...Simply You Are Enough!

Always remember: YOU are your greatest asset! Your greatest asset is not your money, your career, your looks, your car, your house, your status or any other material element. Your greatest asset is you! Your heart, your mind, your body, your soul, your gifts and talents are the attributes that make you the unique individual you are. These are the assets that bring hope and change to the world. These are the gifts that have been nurtured and cultivated by your experiences and your faith in God. They will enable you to leave an indelible footprint in the lives of others.

Now, with your self-esteem revived, realize that you can make the difference you were born to make in this world. You now hold the confidence you needed to be who God called you to be. You can now write that book you've always dreamed of writing, apply for the position you never believed you were qualified for, complete the marathon you always wanted to run, establish a foundation for abused children or start your own business. Whatever ambitions your heart desires, know that you are capable of achieving them. You are a confident, intelligent, ambitious woman with integrity and God given gifts. You have everything you need to walk in your purpose. Don't let anyone tell you otherwise.

Don't ever think that because you don't have an overabundance of "stuff," you are not a valuable asset to God or that you cannot be a beacon of light illuminating the darkness in our world. God doesn't need your "stuff," he wants your heart. God is looking at how you meet the needs of others and love the people you meet every day. He wants your time. He wants you! Why? Because you are his greatest asset. You were created in his likeness and in his image; therefore your presence should be a reflection of his character. How devoted are you are to serving him and living for him? How determined are you to be all he has called you to be and to fulfill your God—given assignment?

Are you asking God about his blueprint for your life? Are you using your God-given gifts and talents to accomplish his plan? When you follow his plan, in his strength, you will leave a permanent imprint in the sand of life that changes the world. What benefit will your gifts and talents be if they remain unused and untapped, lying in a grave once you die? Don't let your assets lay dormant. Lay everything out on the line and live each day as though it were your last on earth. There may not be much time remaining!

It would be a terrible waste to look back years from now and discover you did nothing to make our world a better place. Leave a mark for future generations to remember your story. Live, love, and help heal our world—it is desperately waiting for you. No one knows when his or her time will come to leave this life, but when the time comes, don't you want to know you did everything you could to fulfill your purpose and leave a legacy? Your ultimate reward will be to hear the Lord say, "Well done thou good and faithful servant."

When you were born, God equipped you with everything you needed to fulfill your purpose. Your time, talents and a willing heart is all you need to make a difference. Simply you being yourself is enough!

Affirmation: I am my greatest asset. I am more than the "stuff" I own. I am more than the money I make. I am more than what others think of me. I was born with everything I need to fulfill God's purpose for my life. Simply I am enough!

Action: Describe how you want people to remember you after you are gone. How will you use your gifts and qualities to impact the world?

Despite all these things, overwhelming victory is ours through Christ, who loved us.
Romans 8:37 (NLT)

I know the LORD is always with me. I will not be shaken, for he is right beside me.
Psalm 16:8 (NLT)

The LORD directs the steps of the godly. He delights in every detail of their lives. Though they stumble, they will never fall, for the LORD holds them by the hand.
Psalm 37:23-24 (NLT)

But those who trust in the LORD will find new strength. They will soar high on wings like eagles. They will run and not grow weary. They will walk and not faint.
Isaiah 40:31 (NLT)

Day 30:
Keep On Keepin' On!

This is the last day of our devotions, but the journey to loving yourself and living out God's purpose for your life does not end here. This is a lifelong voyage, requiring commitment and dedication. Don't be afraid to embrace the challenges you will face throughout life. These experiences may cause you to doubt your abilities or self-worth. Issues will arise that cause you to question who you are and why you are here. Popular culture will continue to challenge your definition of beauty.

No matter what, always remember, no one else can define what beauty is to you except you, using God's Word as your guide.

Living in a liberated society has given us the opportunity to express ourselves freely and to walk in our own truth. With this in mind, the definition of beauty lies within your hands. YOU are beauty, elegance, and mystique personified! You are a part of God's magnificent creation. There is no one like you!

There will be days when you aren't feeling your best. Maybe you are grieving over the dissolution of a meaningful relationship, or reeling from the loss of your job. Perhaps it's a bad hair day or you're struggling to get dressed because of a few extra pounds you've gained. These are the waves of life. No matter what you are going through, reflect on your blessings. Remember that your good days have far outweighed your bad days and there is always something to be grateful for.

God is still good. If you need to cry, it's all right to cry. If you need to be alone, then take some time for yourself. If you need to scream, shout, dance, meditate, or any other method of *healthy* therapy, seize the opportunity to release the pain you are feeling. Most important—always turn to God. In him you will find unconditional love, comfort and hope.

I wrote this book to comfort and encourage myself and to bring me through difficult periods in my life. I speak from experience when I say this voyage is ongoing. Every day that I'm alive I consciously choose to go forward by encouraging myself with prayer and daily affirmations. My favorite affirmation is *I was fearfully and wonderfully made in the image of God.* It reminds me that God did not make any mistakes when he created me. I am exactly who he wants me to be. You are exactly who he wants you to be.

No matter what life may bring your way, you are more than a conqueror. If you fall, get up and keep on keepin' on! If you can learn from every experience and challenge, you will continue to grow and you will survive. With God's strength, you will survive. With God's love, you will survive. With God's peace, you will survive. You will survive! You are more than a conqueror!

Affirmation: I am more than a conqueror. I decree and I declare I am victorious in Jesus' name. No matter what comes my way, I will keep on keepin' on!

Action: It's time to celebrate! Treat yourself to dinner, a movie or a new outfit. You deserve it! You've come a long way. If this book has helped you, please pass it on to someone else you think may benefit. If you start to have doubts about who you are, revisit this 30-day journey and allow its message to refill you with the strength you need to continue on.

A Summary . . .

Congratulations on a job well done! Now that you've finished the book, here are some key points to remember about each chapter:

DAY 1: LORD, HELP ME LOVE ME!

Rely on the Lord to carry you through the difficult times you will experience in life.

DAY 2: GET READY FOR WAR

The steps ahead will be challenging, but you can do it. Prepare your mind to face the struggles.

DAY 3: THIS IS YOU NOW

Acknowledge where you are and who you are. Use this as a baseline to determine what you want to accomplish in the future.

DAY 4: THE PAST THAT HAUNTS YOU

Don't let the past prevent you from reaching the future you are supposed to have.

DAY 5: THE PAST THAT HEALS YOU

Use your past to propel you to your future. Learn from its lessons, but don't repeat its mistakes.

Day 6: Forgive Others and Forgive Yourself

Forgiveness fosters healing. Harboring resentment and refusing to let go prevents you from being set free from your pain and hinders forward progression.

Day 7: A Victim of Circumstances ... Or an Overcomer

No more feeling sorry for yourself allowed! Overcome the situation you are dealing with by believing in yourself—and trusting God.

Day 8: Focus on the Positive

There is so much to be grateful for in life. Focus on the good things. They will add value to your life.

Day 9: Acknowledge the Unchangeable

Acknowledge the flaws and features you wish you could change.

Day 10: Accept the Unchangeable

Accept the things you can't change and change the things you can.

Day 11: Deserving of Love

You deserve the love you give yourself. You deserve love because God created you. He loved you enough to send his only son, Jesus, to die on the cross for you. He has a plan and a purpose for your life.

Day 12: Devise a Plan and Follow Through

Devise a set of goals and a plan of action detailing how you will reach your goals for a more confident person with a purpose driven life.

Day 13: Don't Give Up!

No matter how many challenges life brings your way, don't give up. God said he would never put more on you than you can bear. You can make it!

Day 14: Downplay Weaknesses and Build Up Strengths

Appreciate your strongest attributes and favorite features and let them work for you.

Day 15: Take Care of Your Needs

Take time to pamper and nurture yourself. You deserve it.

Day 16: Don't Be a Hater

Don't build yourself up at the expense of others. Encourage others to be the best they can be.

Day 17: Watch What You Watch!

Be mindful of the dangerous and deceiving messages popular culture sends contradicting the Word of God. Meditate on positive and empowering messages.

Day 18: Define Your Beauty

No one else has the right to define what beauty is to you. Create your own definition of beauty, based on God's Word, and work to achieve it.

Day 19: Break Free

You alone can bring yourself out of your current situation. You cannot depend on friends, family or loved ones to make you feel good about who you are, but you *can* do all things through Christ, who strengthens you.

Day 20: Know What You Stand For

You are a woman of integrity and class. Don't settle for anything less than God's best for you.

Day 21: Stay Out of the Mirror

Scrutinizing every flaw and imperfection will destroy your self-image. If you are struggling with the reflection in the mirror, minimize the mirror time until you learn to depend on God's word instead of the image you see in the mirror.

Day 22: Leave Your Mark

You have a responsibility to move beyond your insecurities and begin touching the lives of others. At the end of your life's journey what footprints will you leave behind?

Day 23: No Excuses!

There is no more time to hide behind low self-esteem. The world is depending on you to fulfill your purpose in life.

Day 24: Your Words Have Power

Use the power in your words to build the life you want.

Day 25: Don't Be So Hard on Yourself!

Love yourself unconditionally and set realistic goals and expectations. Don't condemn yourself when you fail. Because of the sacrifice Jesus Christ made by giving his life for us, we are acceptable to God.

Day 26: Find and Be a Mentor/Role Model

Mentoring facilitates growth for the mentor and mentored. Allow someone to encourage and guide you while you encourage and guide someone else.

Day 27: It's Not Your Fault

Sometimes life brings challenges that are out of your control. Rely on God to bring peace and understanding to your spirit when you are going through difficult times.

Day 28: Look How Far You've Come!

You've reached a milestone in your life, and this was no easy feat. Celebrate your accomplishment and appreciate the strength you have within.

Day 29: You Are Your Greatest Asset ...Simply You Are Enough!

Your money, clothes, education and status in life do not define you. Your character, your love for God, your love toward others, and your contribution to humanity will define who you are. Simply you are enough!

Day 30: Keep On Keepin' On!

This voyage isn't over. Remembering where you came from will help keep you on track and get you to where you're going. Never give up. Victory is yours through Christ.

References

Myles Munroe, *"Don't Be a Generational Thief," Your Potential and the Next Generation, Week 48, Day 7. Myles Munroe Devotional & Journal: 365 Days to Realize Your Potential,*

http://books.google.com/books?id=HLhE5vYRMNAC&pg
=PT384&lpg=PT384&dq=myles+munroe+the+graveyard&
source=bl&ots=nAvLQ9mE-f&sig=3UlF-
MhJDaohqj_Wp9r8SIKRM0s&hl=en&sa=X&ei=vam6T4L
WE4f66QHf1KneCg&ved=0CIUBEOgBMAU#v=onepage
&q&f=false (accessed May 21, 2012).

Joshua Henry Jones, *Wisdom for the Soul: Five Millennia of Prescriptions for Spiritual Healing.* Edited by Larry Chang, (Washington: DC, 2006), pg. 615.

For additional information or to schedule workshops, seminars and other speaking engagements please contact the author at:

Attn: Bermesola M Dyer

C/O: BERMIEBEE Publishing, LLC

PO Box 514

Annapolis JCT, MD 20701

Or visit

Website: *www.bermesolamdyer.com*